D0734620

PRAISE FOR NICK VIZZOCA AND WHEN LEADERSHI* HITS THE FAN

"This book presents a unique and innovative approach to developing your leadership style and measuring your leadership effectiveness. The framework helps leaders optimize the balance between productivity and personal / professional satisfaction. Additionally, the personal stories interlaced throughout the book explain the values underlying the framework and keep the reader engaged."

Kevin D. Broom, PhD, MBA
Associate Professor, Vice Chair for Education, and Director of MHA and MHA/MBA Programs, Health Policy and Management, University of Pittsburgh

"Eye-opening … Nick Vizzoca's writing made me both introspective and energized. What is the construct of a happy life, and how can I maximize both my professional and personal success? It's written in a conversational and disarming style that really drives you to critically reevaluate and refocus your goals and aspirations."

Rob DeMichiei
Board Director, Strategic Advisor, Former CFO

"As a university president, I have searched for new ways to work with, encourage, and assess my leadership team to meet the challenges of today and to make us more effective.

Nick Vizzoca has created an assessment instrument for both individual and team leadership development, using a fresh approach to mentoring the next generation of successful and happy leaders. *When Leadershi* Hits the Fan* is a creative path to leadership development and raises the pertinent question of the day: does success bring happiness, or does happiness bring success? Thanks to this book, I'll be raising that question for myself and my team."

Sister Candace Introcaso, CDP, PhD
President, La Roche University

"*When Leadershi* Hits the Fan* provides immediate, actionable insight for leaders of any size company, from start-up to Fortune 100, to better themselves and their teams. Using the tools Nick provides to assess and implement your Personal GDP and Happiness Index is rewarding personally and extends to improved relationships and performance with yourself, your leadership team, and your family."

David Levine
Cofounder and CEO, NuGo Nutrition

"Most of us who set out on a noble cause find the last leg of our journey to be overwhelming. Nick offers an honest approach to finishing strong. His life experiences, ingenuity, gut, and reliance on facts help readers formulate a personal plan to overcome even the greatest challenges.

"After reading, I find myself approaching tough situations with renewed confidence and then sharing the newfound knowledge with many others. Kudos to Nick for putting pen to paper."

Steven Stepp
Founder Managing Partner, Si'Quent Engineering, Architecture & Planning
Senior Executive, Engineering, Advanced Analytics

"Nick Vizzoca delivers a poignant yet pragmatic text that will connect for those who value mission, value their strengths, and most of all value their self-worth! A leadership strategy that clearly has at its core a sense of positivity found in joy, happiness, and pride and that results in meaningful accomplishment. Following the tenets Nick prescribes in his Personal GDP and Personal Happiness Index, a leader can create a team that truly moves forward as one yet allows for difference of opinion that is embraced due to mutual respect.

"In my forty-plus years in management, I am pleased to see this self-perspective take on leadership: lean into your strengths, allow your team to lean into theirs, and have the mission drive the workplan. The results will be meaningful in two ways. First, your team will meet, and likely exceed, the organization's objectives. Second, your team will reach a level of intrinsic satisfaction that produces a vibrant culture others will want to join!"

AJ Harper
President, Healthcare Council of Western Pennsylvania
Adjunct Faculty, Robert Morris University School of Health Services Administration

WHEN LEADERSHI*
HITS THE FAN

WHEN LEADERSHI*
HITS THE FAN

HOW GLOBAL CONCEPTS CAN INFLUENCE
HARD CHOICES AND *INSPIRE GREATNESS*

NICK VIZZOCA

Published by Advantage, Charleston, South Carolina.
Member of Advantage Media Group.

ADVANTAGE is a registered trademark, and the Advantage colophon is a trademark of Advantage Media Group, Inc.

Printed in the United States of America.

10 9 8 7 6 5 4 3 2 1

ISBN: 9781642252484
LCCN: 2021915305

Cover design by Wesley Strickland.
Layout design by Analisa Smith.

This publication is designed to provide accurate and authoritative information in regard to the subject matter covered. It is sold with the understanding that the publisher is not engaged in rendering legal, accounting, or other professional services. If legal advice or other expert assistance is required, the services of a competent professional person should be sought.

Advantage Media Group is proud to be a part of the Tree Neutral® program. Tree Neutral offsets the number of trees consumed in the production and printing of this book by taking proactive steps such as planting trees in direct proportion to the number of trees used to print books. To learn more about Tree Neutral, please visit **www.treeneutral.com**.

Advantage Media Group is a publisher of business, self-improvement, and professional development books and online learning. We help entrepreneurs, business leaders, and professionals share their Stories, Passion, and Knowledge to help others Learn & Grow. Do you have a manuscript or book idea that you would like us to consider for publishing? Please visit **advantagefamily.com**.

I wish to dedicate this book:

To my parents and grandparents, for the sacrifices they made and for taking the chance to make a life in America.

To my sisters, aunts, uncles, and cousins for the support and love that they have given and continue to give.

To the wonderful doctors and nurses who gave me the opportunity to kick cancer's ass and make this book a reality.

To my Italian roots that are firmly planted in America; I am proud of my rich heritage and those who came before me that made my journey possible.

And most of all, to my wife, Marie, and our three wonderful children for their unconditional love and support. Without them, this book may still be sitting somewhere in my head. I love you guys.

CONTENTS

PART 3: PERSONAL HAPPINESS INDEX

"You can't wait until life isn't hard anymore before you decide to be happy."
—*Jane Marczewski, singer / songwriter, three-time cancer survivor*

FOREWORD

BY JOE D'ANDREA

When life comes "full circle," it can be surprising and unexpected. In the case of Nick and me, it is quite a rich, layered, and meaningful tale. It all started in 1984 when I was the Honorary Consul of Italy in Pittsburgh. In my capacity as consul, I handled many details pertaining to legal documents that were needed by Italian citizens in the area, as I was familiar with the needs and lives of immigrants from Italy since I had left my Italian roots in my teens.

Nick's father Luciano Vizzoca, who had previously immigrated to America, stopped in to see me at my office. My interaction with him was brief but memorable, and I went back to my duties, never realizing that our lives would intertwine approximately thirty-five years later.

In late 2019, my wife Gloria's declining health necessitated a move to a skilled nursing facility. Not wanting to live separately, I decided to move into the independent living facility with her. As fate would have it, the CEO of that senior community where Gloria and I moved was no other than Luciano Vizzoca's son, Nicola (Nick).

I have had the pleasure of getting to know Nick and have witnessed firsthand his dedication to leading an organization with care, compassion, and empathy. In my role as the Honorary Consul of Italy in Pittsburgh, I have traveled the world and met numerous dignitaries and leaders. Upon watching Nick lead, I often enjoyed seeing similarities to some of those leaders. Like them, Nick has a passion for leadership, and his management skills are dynamic. Employees thrive in the culture that he has built, and there is an environment of positivity. I watched Nick hustle as he navigated his team through the COVID-19 pandemic and was cognizant of his leadership as he reassured families that the care of the clients in his facilities was paramount. His business acumen renders me awestruck.

In his book, Nick shares prescriptive ways to embrace and tighten the talents and skills that you were given in life. By doing so, you can indeed create a life that is deserving of your hard work. Likewise, I see Nick using his innate skills and talents to create an environment where all residents and staff feel valued and cared for. Under his direction, the organization has grown through strategically planned acquisitions and collaborations, and he has assembled a team that is one of the best in the industry. He has made a difference in the community and shares his knowledge with others.

There is a lesson for all of us: those who you meet during your life's journeys may leave and then reenter your life at a moment's notice. Plus, those whom you help in life may end up helping you—not that you expect this; it just happens that way.

Luciano and I have very much enjoyed our reacquaintance. We have nightly chats and discuss everything from our lives—from memories of our old mountain villages to current issues in America. It is my great honor to call both Luciano and Nick my dear friends and my great honor to present to you this book, which will guide you to reach deep inside yourself to find your skills and your passion, and then use them to find your life's work, your life's purpose, and most importantly, happiness.

—Giuseppe Fernando Paolo (Joseph) D'Andrea was born in Roccamandolfi, Molise, Italy, in 1929. As a young man during World War II, he bore witness to wartime destruction, losing friends and neighbors as his family gave shelter to indigent soldiers returning home as well as a Jewish family in hiding. After immigrating to the US in 1948, he earned degrees from Duquesne University and the University of Mexico, as well as his master's in education at the University of Pittsburgh. He is a former President of the Pennsylvania State Education Association, founded the American Italian Cultural Institute, and served at the Italian Consulate in Pittsburgh from 1983 to 1999.

CHOOSE YOUR HARD ... BY GIVING A DAMN

No one has ever done anything great by just doing the same things the same way. No one great has earned their place in the world because they did things the easy way. I dare you to name someone who has.

Life is hard, right? We've all heard it—from our parents, from bosses, from mentors and friends; it's just another fact of life. But the type of hard we are faced with changes throughout life:

During the early years, maybe you said, "Tying my shoes is hard," or "Reading is hard."

During the teenage and college years, maybe it was "Breaking up is hard," or "Practice is hard."

As an adult, it turns into "Job interviewing is hard," or "Meeting goals is hard."

The two that will change your life forever are "Marriage is hard" and "Parenting is hard."

Any of these sound familiar?

In the end, life is a series of choosing one "hard" over another. Learning to read is hard, yeah ... but so is being illiterate. Being single is hard … and so is being married. Doing your job well is hard, but so is being unemployed.

The hard you choose helps determine the level of greatness you can ultimately achieve.

But choosing your hard doesn't have to be arbitrary—in fact, it should be anything but arbitrary. Instead of playing eeny, meeny, miney, mo, you can learn how to gauge your psyche, take stock of your mental and physical tools, your capacity to tolerate stress, and then choose the hard that can lead to real happiness and success.

I don't believe in sugarcoating things. Not with my employees, not with my kids, and certainly not with myself. But with each of these "hards" in life, I tend to shrug my shoulders, chuckle, and meet them with the same reply: "No shit, it's hard!"

And yes, I say that to my kids, too.

It's only when something is hard that you can truly appreciate and enjoy the rewards of getting through it. If any of these were easy, then how would you ever appreciate the rewards of getting through each "hard"? The hard you choose helps determine the level of greatness you can ultimately achieve.

In your career, the *hard* evolves as you attempt to measure your successes, but not having successes to measure is also hard. So I ask, which hard do you choose? Because you *do* have a choice. You have the ability to choose which *hard* you're going to pursue. One *hard* leads to rewards and happiness … and the other to lost opportunities of what might have been and life lessons.

It's a common misconception that happiness and difficulty are opposites, but they are actually linked in a powerful way. The greater difficulty you overcome, the more possible reward, the more possible happiness. In a way, when you choose your *hard*, you're also choosing your *happy*.

MEASURING YOURSELF

Throughout my life, I've been surrounded by people who knew how to choose their hard, so I'm sure that's why I gravitate toward those same types of people in my work. As important as it is to know how to choose your *hard*, that's just the beginning of the work. One thing I wished I'd learned earlier is that you don't have to be the CEO of a Fortune 500 company to be a success. And I know I'm not alone in that because we live in a world that thrives on benchmarks of the world's richest and most powerful, where people think you need to be on a list of some sort to be successful, like "Thirty under Thirty." But I've come to realize over time that's a narrow view of success. Why don't we have a "Sixty over Sixty" list? Is success not allowed there?

Hell, I've learned more about success and happiness from eighty-year-olds than I ever did from a thirty-year-old millionaire. But more on that later.

Before we can even attempt to measure success, we need to measure ourselves. Now, maybe you're thinking, "What in the world do you mean, measure ourselves?" But stay with me for a second and think about this: would you start leading any endeavor without first knowing what strengths and tangibles you possess to make that endeavor successful? You know it's going to be hard going in, but why make it harder by not being prepared? It would be the equivalent of a contractor showing up to the worksite without any tools or heavy-duty equipment.

Early in this process for measuring myself, I was thinking through what makes a good leader and asking, "How are leaders made?" The more I read popular leadership literature, the more I was bombarded with what leadership traits and attributes I needed to attain to be a successful leader. It was all "Twelve Ways to Be This" and "Nine Steps to Success." While there was certainly some wisdom there, it was mentally exhausting to keep up with it all. For me, this resulted in a lot of confusion about the definition of a successful leader—in the middle of all the advice of "You have to be this or you have to be that," all I could hear was "You can't be yourself."

In other words, you end up making a Frankenstein's monster—or "Leaderstein," I guess—built from pieces of someone else's ideals and standards. In a moment of clarity, I thought to myself, "Why are these so-called leadership experts telling others how to act or what they need to be successful and how to be happy? Isn't happiness subjective? Doesn't that mean success might also be subjective?"

Instead of measuring success by someone else's standard, I think you have to first take a step back and reflect on who *you* are. For example, if you can't skate, you're probably not going to go be a pro hockey player, no matter how much you enjoy the game. Sorry if that bursts your bubble … but instead of trying to be something you're not, be something that you are. If you have an artistic mind instead of a scientific one, that's all right! Leaning into your strengths is one of the best ways to make sure you've chosen the right *hard*, no matter what it is.

So if success means different things to different people, then how do you start to measure it? In leadership, measuring success is often misconstrued and confused with accumulation of wealth, authority, and power. But measuring success in these terms alone can be deceptive because it only shows one side of the story—what you can fit on a piece of paper in a report. You might be a rock star to the shareholders—but maybe the whole company thinks you're a self-centered jerk only worried about your own status. Even if you're not a jerk, financial reports can't measure how you *feel* about your work, your level of passion or satisfaction. In other words, numbers can give the impression of success, but without the feeling of success coming from the work and your convictions, do you really believe in what you're doing?

In short, the popular leadership advice out there is being given blindly and without really helping people understand their strengths, aspirations, goals, and passions. People and evaluation tools are being used to build a new cookie-cutter culture—and leader—based on a set of traits.

What the heck are we doing? I don't know about you, but I don't want to be something I'm not. I think we are all unique and we each bring a different set of attributes to the table, so someone telling me how to act or what to say is not going to make me happy—or successful.

So I stopped and thought, "There needs to be a different approach. Instead of telling people how to act and what they need to be or do, we should be asking people to first identify their strengths, level of engagement, and levels of happiness." This is true for individuals, managers, teams, and organizations.

Whether it's our own personal leadership aspirations, team goals, or organizational goals, we must always start somewhere. It makes sense to start by identifying the measures of our self-tangibles (God-given abilities and talents), aligning your purpose with your contentment (what brings you happiness), and then utilizing those measures as we journey along our paths.

A NEW CONCEPT

When I started to think about this in terms of my own leadership journey, I asked myself, "If we can measure the tangible economic output and strength of a country through GDP, can we apply the same concept to people? Could there be such a thing as a personal GDP? And what if I could measure that in a meaningful way that will help me become a better leader?"

While you probably know what GDP is, you might not be as familiar with something called the United Nations Sustainable Development Solutions Network. This is a department of the UN that measures countries, not by their economic output, but by their level of happiness, determined through measuring various life factors. Both GDP and the Happiness Index are vital to understanding a country and what makes it successful, so why not do the same with people? Why not look at individuals, teams, and organizations as countries within countries?

After this brainstorm, I wanted to look at how to incorporate these measures and focus on the core of an individual, team, or organization by combining happiness and personal strengths. Being strong in one measure and not the other does not assure success—instead, the goal is to be as balanced as possible to ensure long-term success. Hence, the concepts of *Personal* Gross Domestic Product and *Personal* Happiness Index were born.

Yes, this is a new concept, but it's one that I think will help all of us begin to think differently about our careers, our teams, and our organizations. Understanding our **Personal GDP (P-GDP)** and our **Personal Happiness Index (P-HI)** forms the foundation necessary to allow us to then measure our true successes.

I've loved baseball my whole life, so you need to prepare yourself now for lots of sports analogies, especially baseball. One day, I was watching an interview with Cody Bellinger of the Dodgers before a game during the 2020 World Series. They asked him, "Cody, does success bring happiness or does happiness bring success for you?"

And Cody took a step back and answered, "Wow. I never thought about that. But honestly, happiness brings success."

He couldn't be more right.

It may sound simple, but it is indeed profound. This thought commences our understanding on how to measure leadership in terms of Personal GDP and Happiness Index—if you can identify and understand your strengths in light of your satisfaction and passion, then you can apply the same principles to your team and then your organization. You can see this happening in a series of linked steps: measuring your Personal GDP and Personal Happiness Index, measuring your team's GDP and Happiness Index, and then measuring your organization's GDP and Happiness Index.

For this to work, I think you also have to figure out what your values are because not only do they provide a lens to focus your own strengths and happiness, but they also provide a lens for you to find like-minded people for your team. Values aren't usually something you can force someone to develop—they are not a list of attributes or traits, but rather they are individualized. And they are typically developed over the course of your life, shaped by your experiences, whether it's the hard that you have chosen, or the hard that has chosen you—that is, adversity. When it comes down to it, that's exactly what adversity is: any event where the you-know-what hits

> **There are three values in particular that I look for in all my team members: the Spirit of the Immigrant, the Heart of the Warrior, and the Soul of the Servant.**

the fan. For me, there are three values in particular that I look for in all my team members: the **Spirit of the Immigrant**, the **Heart of the Warrior**, and the **Soul of the Servant**.

THE SPIRIT OF THE IMMIGRANT

My parents and grandparents immigrated to the United States from Italy in the late '60s with the idea of making a better life for themselves and their families through opportunities and a spirit of optimism and community. Understanding that it would be hard, they decided to choose that hard and chase their dreams. The risk and uncertainty were there, yes, but so was the potential for reward and happiness.

I was born when they were all living in the South Oakland neighborhood of Pittsburgh; my early years were spent in the same stomping grounds as icons like pop artist Andy Warhol, Hall of Famer Dan Marino, and wrestling legend Bruno Sammartino. Our tight-knit neighborhood was like the Little Italy of Pittsburgh, so I grew up thinking of myself as Italian, not American. It wasn't until we moved to the suburbs when I was five that I realized not everyone spoke Italian. My first days of school, I was bullied for my accent, my homemade clothes, and even the food I would bring for lunch.

Thanks to the Spirit of the Immigrant I saw in my parents—and thanks to my teacher Mrs. Wolfe, who was willing to spend the extra time with me—I was able to embrace that *hard* and work through it to master the English language.

THE HEART OF THE WARRIOR

I wish I could say the rest of my childhood was smooth sailing after those initial struggles with school, but that wouldn't be the truth. At the age of twelve, life threw me another curve ball—I was diagnosed with Stage III Hodgkin's Lymphoma.

So there I was at twelve years old, facing major surgery to remove a grapefruit-sized tumor from my chest followed by twelve rounds of chemotherapy and twenty-four rounds of radiation therapy for good measure. Sounds terrifying, right?

Treatment lasted from eight in the morning till six at night, then I would go home and throw up until about three in the morning because I couldn't keep anything down. That's just what chemo does. But I vividly remember one night, lying there, and my mother was in a rocking chair next to me and wouldn't leave my side, keeping a cold compress on my forehead. She didn't care that she wasn't getting any sleep—she was going to be right beside me all through the night, fighting for me.

Being surrounded by that kind of unconditional love and deep compassion had a profound and surprising effect on me. I felt like I couldn't show my mother how much I was hurting, how the treatment was tearing me up inside, because then she might feel like she was failing, and I couldn't let her think that for a moment. Instead of simply absorbing her love and fighting spirit, I was reflecting it back to her. I could see the toll it was taking on her and my family and the sacrifices they were making to be there for me. My concern for them made me want to fight, and, incredibly, I found that I wasn't afraid to go through it.

This Heart of the Warrior is the drive to fight for other people, no matter what. Anyone will fight for themselves when survival instinct kicks in—but a warrior willingly chooses the hard and faces danger knowing it's for the good of others. I know for a fact that fighting cancer at such a young age helped me become the leader I am today. Adversity will always change your perspective. For me, it's helped me put the big picture in perspective and not sweat the small stuff because life is short. As the old saying goes, it taught me not to miss the forest for the trees and to celebrate the small battles on the way to winning the war.

THE SOUL OF THE SERVANT

I always had aspirations to become a CEO, but honestly, I had no mindset to enter the field of senior care. I'd chased money for a while by working for an insurance company and found I didn't care for it. Then I shifted to ICU operations even though I'd be taking a pay cut, but I felt good about how my work there could impact patients and families going through terrible situations, especially given my own cancer experience. The selflessness of the doctors, nurses, and clinicians has stuck with me to this day.

Many religious communities have a special tradition of conducting a mass to welcome aboard new leaders for their ministries. When I became CEO, this was very, very emotional for me, because it hammered home the fact that my role, first and foremost, was to be a servant to the people they were entrusting me with. I was there to serve our residents, their families, and the team working under me. Period.

It sounds counterintuitive, but as a leader, you have to see yourself as the first servant of the organization. Serving and leading seem like opposing ideas, but serving your team is really an opportunity to show people that they are valued. And when people feel valued, they value you as their leader and *want* to follow. The Soul of the Servant inspires others to give the best of themselves in their service—and everyone is happier for it.

YOUR TURN

These three values have shaped so much of my life as a person, my decision-making, how I measure my strengths and happiness, and how I choose my *hard*. Whether you share those values or not, they are the reasons *I* give a damn.

Look, I'm not an expert on you. I can't know your experiences, your values, your strengths, or what makes you happy. So I'm not going to start listing off "Eighteen Skills Every Leader Masters" and "Nine Habits of Every Successful Leader." If you're looking for that book, it's not this one. Sorry, but not sorry.

Like I said at the start, you get to choose your hard—you can go into the office every day and do the same BS routine, deal with the same problems, the same dissatisfaction, and just white-knuckle it until retirement—or you can choose to see this as a chance to reset and regroup, to learn how to measure yourself first, and then harness those measures to build a greater leader, happier team, and better organization.

Measuring leadership in this way is going to be hard because it's going to demand that you be honest with yourself, and you're probably going to hear some things that you don't want to hear. I'm not going to beat around the bush or sugarcoat things, but I can promise you this: as hard as it is, it's going to be easier than looking back at a catalogue of regrets, burnt bridges, and unhappiness.

Choosing the right hard is important because, if it hasn't happened to you already—spoiler alert—you're going to be faced with adversity, and when shi* hits the fan, the hard choices you make afterward are going to determine whether it gets cleaned up or makes a bigger mess. How you handle adversity is what separates the truly great leaders from those who are leaders in name only.

So it's your turn now. You can choose leadership or leadershi* ... both are choices, and both are hard, but only one leads to success and happiness. No one's going to choose for you.

PART 1
A NEW VIEW

CHAPTER 1

INTRODUCING PERSONAL GDP AND PERSONAL HAPPINESS INDEX

Through money and power, you cannot solve problems.
Problems must be solved through the human heart.
— *DALAI LAMA*

For the first few years of my life, I didn't even know I was American. In the South Oakland neighborhood of Pittsburgh, I lived in a tight-knit community filled by my parents, my grandparents, aunts and uncles, and all their fellow Italian immigrants. I may have been born in the US, sure, but everyone around me spoke Italian, ate Italian, and lived Italian.

I can't speak for all immigrant neighborhoods, but ours felt like a country unto itself. Everyone focused on the strengths and talents they brought with them to help build a stronger community. For example, my mother with a sewing machine was like Beethoven with a piano, making drapes, slipcovers, clothes, and alterations. And then there was my grandmother who was great with kids and would watch us so that Mom could create masterpieces uninterrupted. And don't forget my uncle the winemaker. I mean, every community needs a winemaker, right?

One of the many things I admire about the immigrants' spirit is their ability to hone in on their strengths and make themselves indispensable to the community. Everybody had a role in that village. They knew their role, excelled in it, and allowed others to do the same. No one there came to America and said, "Well, I've changed countries, so now I need to change myself. I'm really good at mechanics, but what the heck, I should become a stockbroker." No, they came for the freedom to grow and expand the skills they already had."

> **When everyone gets to focus on their unique talents and strengths, it only makes the team stronger.**

Too often, leaders fall into the trap of trying to be the expert on everything instead of focusing on their individual strengths and helping others find their strengths. When everyone gets to focus on their unique talents and strengths, it only makes the team stronger.

It's the same in sports—successful teams pick players because they fill roles when they want to win. Spending a quarter of a billion dollars on players doesn't make a great team. The money means nothing if you can't get some wins to back it up. But occasionally, some owners become more concerned with selling tickets, so they spend millions getting stars on the team, not thinking about whether those players will work together well. But that's not really how you build a team—instead, you wind up with a group of individuals playing for themselves.

As a CEO, it's no different on my team. Viewing my team as its own community, its own country, I don't need a bunch of clones.

Instead, I need people to fill roles—whether it's writing, data analysis, or predictive modeling—and then the sum of those parts will come together as a whole, each person exercising their individual strength to make the best team I could ask for.

Now, let's be honest with each other. Even if you know what you're passionate about, not everyone knows their strengths right off the bat. Some people may not even know the right size of bat they need to be swinging—too big and they can't see around it … too small and they can't cover the entire strike zone—otherwise known as the Goldilocks principle. Sometimes you learn what your strengths are by process of elimination when your weaknesses come to light. And there's nothing wrong with that so long as it moves you the right direction.

I always knew I wanted to work in healthcare to help others, especially after my cancer fight when I was twelve. Outside of my family, those doctors, nurses, and clinicians were my heroes, so I figured I should become a doctor. But my freshman year as a pre-med student really handed my ass to me, and I quickly realized that I was not cut out to become a doctor. I learned that it took a special person and a very scientific and disciplined type of mind that I simply didn't possess.

That didn't deter me from healthcare, though. It just made me understand I needed to find a different way in—one that would benefit from the gifts that I *did* possess. The problem is that a lot of people equate strengths with passions, and they give up at the first sign of weakness instead of exploring the other options available that they might excel in.

These are the people who think the only way to enjoy baseball is to play it. But then they find out that they're lousy at pitching and swinging a bat. They forget that baseball teams need coaches, and scouts, and managers, and the guy selling beer in the stands. *Especially* the guy selling beer. Who's to say one person has less passion for the sport just because of the role they are filling? And who's to say one person's job is less or more important?

Knowing your role doesn't mean settling for second best. It means finding your strengths so that you can contribute to whatever it is you're most passionate about. Instead of focusing on the *can't*s in your life, that is, what you *can't* do, it means shifting to focus to the *cans*, what you *can* do. I believe this ability to focus on the *cans* over the *can'ts* is an essential mindset for any leader.

The "Aha!" moment for me in measuring myself as a leader was when I started thinking of myself as a country and then, by extension, thinking of my team as a country. This concept focuses on leadership self-evaluation by combining two measures that already exist to evaluate both the economic strength and the happiness of nations. I discovered that, by taking these measures and applying them to individuals, it allows them to understand what matters most to them: their passion and purpose.

It also creates focus on the core of how to become a leader by putting that passion and purpose together with happiness in light of one's personal economic sustainability and viability—their strengths and abilities. It's not about choosing one over the other but balancing the two to identify a route to long-term success and happiness.

INTRODUCING PERSONAL GDP

In the world of economics, one of the most used measures of a country's strength and prosperity is its Gross Domestic Product (GDP). In its simplest definition, GDP uses a variety of factors to measure the total monetary or market value of all the finished goods and services produced within a country's borders in a specific timeframe. Those factors are cumulatively used to provide a comprehensive scorecard that assesses the economic strength and viability of the country.

Although the factors determining economic health (those that include dollar values associated with them) are essential, it's also necessary to look at one important factor that is *limiting* the nation's economic growth. While there are several methods to determine a nation's GDP[1], the five basic factors are:

Natural Resources

Health and Infrastructure (or lack thereof)

Human Capital

Technology

Productivity

Think about this for a second: if economists can measure a country's economic health through these factors and they place a ton of value on those findings, then why can't we do the same for an individual? Why can't it serve as a scorecard for not only existing leaders but as a benchmark for aspiring leaders? Why not take these same five factors and adapt them to people, teams, and organizations?

The term I've coined for this idea is **Personal Gross Domestic Product**, or **P-GDP**. Each of the factors used to measure GDP can be adapted to measure the strength of a person. Eventually, you will then be able to adapt your P-GDP to determine your **T-GDP** (**Team GDP**) and **O-GDP** (**Organizational GDP**), but we've got to start with ourselves before we scale it up for our teams and organizations.

Now, a word of caution: this measure is not the sole determining factor in evaluating success or, more importantly, finding a person's purpose, passion, and ultimate happiness. Once P-GDP is determined, it should be combined with the second concept that I will introduce later. It is but one half of the picture.

---

1   Some include the income approach and the expenditure approach.

In Part II, we'll go a lot more in depth on each of these factors, but for now, we need to at least understand the basics from a 35,000-foot view.

NATURAL RESOURCES

Exactly as it sounds, these are any resources that naturally occur within the geographic boundaries of the country and can either benefit the country's people directly or be sold as goods. Likewise, every person alive also has natural resources available to them, things that occur naturally provided from birth. It could be athletic talent, a sense of humor, people skills, an analytical mind, prolific writing ability, and so on.

Now, here is where I say each of these measures is independent but contributes to make up the whole. Not all countries have the same naturally-occurring resources, just like not all people are born with the same set of personal natural resources. But that does not stop a country from succeeding, nor should it stop an individual from doing the same. Instead of comparing ourselves to one another and bitching about what we *don't* have, it's about focusing on harnessing what you *do* have.

What are your natural, God-given abilities? What makes you unique? What are you able to do that no one else around you can do as well as you can?

HEALTH AND INFRASTRUCTURE (OR LACK THEREOF)

This measure of GDP assesses not the growth of an economy but a limitation to economic growth. Although not directly related to economic growth in terms of the ability to generate dollars, poor health and lack of adequate infrastructure can limit a nation's potential for growth.

In early 2020, the world was brought to a halt by a pandemic that devastated economies through the inability to conduct business. You might have heard about it. This event clearly demonstrated the effect that health can have on an economy. Within P-GDP, **Health** is just as significant. A person who is mentally and physically healthy can better focus on their purpose and will therefore be much more effective as a leader. In fact, this is so important to me personally that I have created a health and wellness category within my annual goals in my review with our board of directors. Also, I believe a person's health goes beyond just physical health and also encompasses financial, spiritual, and mental health.

Likewise, **Infrastructure**—or its lack—relates directly to whether a nation can grow and progress. A prime example of this is Sierra Leone in West Africa where most of the roads are still the ones the British constructed before the country gained independence in 1961. But in 2016, the country opened its first major highway in its modern history and subsequently saw its GDP rise over the following years, partly due to having this new method to move people and goods across the nation.

With P-GDP, I see Infrastructure in terms of whether you have the tools and resources you need to act upon your natural resources. You may have the greatest arm in the world, but if you don't have a football to throw to prove it, then what's the point?

So where might you be lacking in Health? Is it your physical health? Mental health? Do you have the tools and Infrastructure you need to exercise your natural resources to be more productive? If not, how can you change that?

HUMAN CAPITAL

Of the five factors measured in GDP, **Human Capital** is one that a country as well as an individual can harness when it's properly recognized. In essence, Human Capital refers to the knowledge, skill sets, and experience that workers possess. So it's not just a question of whether workers are available but whether the *right* workers are available with the *right* skills.

These skills and knowledge provide economic value to a country given that a skilled and knowledgeable workforce can potentially lead to increased productivity. Within GDP, this measure is done through the very high level of looking at how educated or not educated a workforce is, or it can be based on measurements of trade skills and experience. The theory is that the more skills and education a worker has, the better they will be at their task. Also, a more skilled worker should have the ability to learn something new as their job evolves or even drive innovation through their knowledge and skills.

With P-GDP, this is where you need to take inventory of your personal skills and knowledge. Unlike human capital measured in GDP, you must also take inventory of your interests to help determine your P-GDP.

How can you take those skills and knowledge and apply them to what brings you a series of joys and personal satisfaction? Are you investing time in growing your Human Capital in the areas that interest you most?

TECHNOLOGY

According to *Science Direct*, "Technological transformation causes an increase in the capita per person and motivates savings and investments and as a result, causes an increase to real GDP. If technological transformation ceases, the growth will also stop."[2] It's obvious why this is an essential factor for countries—the more access to technology a country has, the greater impact it can have on their economic output.

But **Technology** is also incredibly important when assessing your P-GDP. Within P-GDP, technological capabilities are both high tech *and* low tech. In this view, **Low Tech** is the human touch and **High Tech** exists to reinforce Low Tech, not replace it.

For example, I work in an industry—specifically senior healthcare—where technological advancements are made every day. Whether in research, treatment, or prevention, technology plays a large role in the delivery of high-quality care. But at the core of healthcare is human interaction, which is a no-tech solution. Our facilities could have the greatest equipment known to mankind, but if our workers don't *care* about our seniors, then that's going to show in the care, or rather, lack thereof.

This human interaction is not just applicable to healthcare but all industries and all jobs. How do you treat people? How do you communicate with people? And I'm not talking about your ability to text or use social media. It's not about being tech-savvy but human-savvy.

PRODUCTIVITY

Finally, productivity is the measure of a country's workforce in terms of their unemployment rate, how much of the labor force is employed, and what is available based on the needs within the country. It is the end result, the peak, of every factor that comes before it. As we relate that to P-GDP, we look beyond the simple facts of whether you are employed and can remain employed to what the felt impact is of the work that is done. In other words, it's not just about doing great work

---

2   Hülya Kesici Çalışkan, "Technological Change and Economic Growth," *Procedia: Social and Behavioral Sciences* 195 (2015): 651.

… it's about *feeling* great about that work because you believe in it.

Many countries have a very strong labor force and will score well in that metric, but I think you have to look deeper and assess the *engagement* of that workforce too. It's the same for you as you gauge your Productivity—how engaged are you in your work?

Personally, you may have a secure job within a very strong field, but does that transfer to being satisfied or happy in the job? Does your job evoke excitement that makes you love what you do and, in turn, makes you as productive as possible? How engaged are you in the work day to day?

When we look at true **Productivity**, we look beyond the task list of what you have to do every day, digging deep into whether you are doing the right things and whether it will have a lasting impact. It means being able to refocus on how you made a difference in someone's life through your work and finding the motivation to get through the hard days and inspire productivity in others.

INTRODUCING PERSONAL HAPPINESS INDEX

My wife and I joke all the time that the happiest time of our life was after the birth of our son; I was working, she was a new stay-at-home mom, we had a whopping twenty cents in the checking account, it would be a Tuesday, and payday wasn't till Friday. The money didn't matter, though—we were happy.

You've heard it before, but I'm going to say it again: money can't buy happiness. I was initially making a bit less as a CEO than when I was working in ICU operations, but I was happier because I got to do something every day that I was passionate about and that utilized my unique skills and values.

There's a quote I love that's often attributed to John Lennon:

"When I was five, my mother always told me happiness was the key to life. When I went to school, they asked me what I wanted to do when I grew up. I wrote down 'happy.' They told me I didn't understand the assignment, and I told them they didn't understand life."

Being a successful leader involves more than just understanding your tangible strengths and output as measured by your P-GDP—it must also include your **Personal Happiness Index**, or **P-HI**. To keep us from any confusion as I introduce this part of the concept, it's important for me to define happiness as separate from the feeling of joy. I define happiness as a state of being that persists over an extended period, whereas I see joy as a sudden burst of happiness that lasts for a small amount of time.

Besides GDP, another measure that is conducted annually is the overall happiness of a country and the people that reside there. There are many factors that take into consideration a country's overall happiness and well-being. Most people, including myself, want to believe that they are generally happy with their lives, but what are we basing our happiness on?

Taking this concept and applying it to a person and their individual situation allows you to objectively measure if you truly are happy.

According to the Gallup World Poll, the method used for ranking a nation's level of happiness index is called the Cantril Self-Anchoring Striving Scale. The following are some of the measures used to determine a country's overall happiness:

Health Life Expectancy
Social Support
Positive Affect
Negative Affect
Freedom
Generosity

For our purposes, I'm eliminating Health Life Expectancy as a factor since it is a measure of factual data based on birth and death rates. Doesn't really work here, though I hope you live as long as possible. But the other five factors can absolutely be utilized to help us understand where we land on our own Personal Happiness Index.

SOCIAL SUPPORT

As an extension of the Health measure within P-GDP, **Social Support** asks the questions, "Do you have a good support system in times of need? If you need support, do you have relatives or friends you can count on?"

For me personally, a strong network of professionals, mentors, family, and friends played a significant role in the search for my passion and happiness. As I progressed in my journey, I found the best support came from my wife and children, who have always been my biggest supporters.

Surrounding yourself with a strong network gives you the best chance at personal and professional success. Not just yes-men and women but people who will give you brutal honesty and call you out when necessary. It's become a rule of thumb for me to "trust only those who can be honest with you." When I first became CEO, I would purposefully say certain things just to see who would agree with me or who would stand up and tell me, "Nick, you're crazy." I wanted people on my team who cared enough about the success of the company to push back if they saw me headed the wrong direction. That's *real* support.

Also, this isn't a popularity contest. It's not about seeing how many followers you can collect like a social media celebrity. Social Support is about quality, not quantity; depth, not breadth. Who cares about the same things you care about? Who will fight *with* you and alongside you?

POSITIVE AFFECT

To paraphrase the late Coach Jim Valvano, "If you can laugh, think, and be brought to tears today, you have had a full day." The ability to have a **Positive Affect** is defined as the average of three measures: happiness, laughter, and enjoyment.

We all have situations that arise that challenge us and are out of our control, but I always try to find the positive in every situation. You may not have your dream job yet, but you can make the choice to find something you enjoy in your job. And not to sound like a broken record, but happiness is a choice, specifically, making the choice to look past a difficult moment and find something to be happy about. Having a Positive Affect is also a choice, and it can be developed through practice.

As important as it is to pinpoint what brings you happiness, laughter, and enjoyment, it's more important to figure out how to wield a Positive Affect to bring about happiness, laughter, and enjoyment in others to help them through their hard days.

NEGATIVE AFFECT

Not to be Captain Obvious here, but the opposite of a Positive Affect is a **Negative Affect,** which is defined as the average of three measures: worry, sadness, and anger.

I come from a long line of worriers, so it's wired into my DNA. The fact that I work in healthcare and have seen death and challenges has provided me plenty of opportunity for both sadness and anger. But in P-HI, we look at how a Negative Affect can also be a good thing when put in balance with a Positive Affect.

It's about being able to use negativity as fuel for change and growth, about being cautiously pessimistic in a way that protects your team and helps you make calculated risks. A healthy dose of Negative Affect can actually push you in a positive direction. An excess of it makes you a miserable human to be around, unable to inspire or encourage others.

FREEDOM

In a lot of countries, it can be easy to take freedom for granted, which is why this factor is so critical. I have been in many roles throughout my life where I worked for *bosses*, not *leaders*—there's a big difference between the two. Bosses gave me the perception of freedom, but in reality, I only had the freedom to agree with them or do what they said.

I've learned that as a leader, I have the ability to help others achieve happiness based upon the freedom I give to them. Do they feel the freedom to speak their mind? Do they feel the freedom to make decisions on their own instead of running to me with every little problem? I'd rather have to say, "Whoa!" to my staff than "Giddy up!" Taking initiative is a sign of felt freedom.

Taking initiative is a sign of felt freedom.

In P-HI, **Freedom** isn't about just doing whatever you want to do. Instead, it should result in accountability, a sense of ownership, and inclusion. Are you satisfied or dissatisfied with your Freedom to choose what you do with your life? If you're a leader, are you providing Freedom to others to pursue success?

GENEROSITY

For me, the idea of giving something to another human being is extremely gratifying. I always say to my children that I love giving gifts rather than receiving them. That is why I believe **Generosity** is the pinnacle of one's happiness.

The problem is, not enough people practice it. Sometimes people feel as though they should only be the recipient because they do not have the financial means to give, but generosity can also mean giving your time and talent. When you can honestly recognize and appreciate all that you've been blessed to receive, then it becomes natural to want to pay that forward.

I see Generosity as the overflow that occurs when you have a strong Social Support, a balanced Positive and Negative Affect, and the Freedom to pursue happiness. In the classic story *A Christmas Carol*, Ebenezer Scrooge's happiness went hand in hand with him learning to be generous in his time, talent, and treasure.

While I probably won't hang out with some ghosts in my nightgown like Scrooge, I do look for ways to donate my time, talent, and treasure—and I ask my team to do the same, not as a chore or out of guilt, but to give to something that they feel passionate about and brings them happiness and fulfillment.

BRINGING IT TOGETHER

So now that we have introduced the concepts of P-GDP as well as your P-HI, you may say to yourself, "Okay, so now what?" I would argue that if you are able to identify your strengths and weaknesses through P-GDP and couple that with your P-HI, you will find your purpose and be able to start taking the steps to make it your passion.

Achieving economic strength and happiness together is not as easy as it sounds. Despite knowing that money can't buy happiness, I fell into the trap of thinking that leadership meant making the most money and having the power to tell others what to do. Having learned otherwise through experience, I want to be clear that becoming a leader for the wrong reasons will not lead to happiness.

To prove this, let's go back to GDP and the World Happiness Index. The following shows the ranking of the largest, most powerful countries in today's world economy based on their GDP for 2020.

GROSS DOMESTIC PRODUCT RANKINGS 2020[3]

1. United States
2. China
3. Japan
4. Germany
5. United Kingdom
6. India
7. France
8. Italy
9. Canada
10. S. Korea

Now, the question is this: does the economic strength of these countries guarantee happiness among their people? To answer that, let's look at the list that ranks the happiest countries in the world based on the measures we reviewed earlier.

---

3   Knoema. "World GDP Ranking 2020, GDP by Country, Data and Charts," accessed 4/2/2021, https://knoema.com/nwnfkne/world-gdp-ranking-2020-gdp-by-country-data-and-charts.

THE 10 HAPPIEST COUNTRIES IN THE WORLD IN 2020[4]

1. Finland (43rd in GDP)
2. Iceland (105th in GDP)
3. Denmark (35th in GDP)
4. Switzerland (20th in GDP)
5. Netherlands (18th in GDP)
6. Sweden (22nd in GDP)
7. Germany (4th in GDP)
8. Norway (28th in GDP)
9. New Zealand (50th in GDP)
10. Austria (27th in GDP)

Notice that only Germany makes both lists. Which makes me wonder if stocking up on some German chocolates might just be the key to having the best of both worlds. In fact, the other nine countries on the list of happiest countries did not even make the top 15 for GDP. Lesson learned: money and power cannot buy happiness.

Instead, happiness has a value that surpasses economic understanding. If you work hard enough at your passion, you will find that you will make more than enough money and be respected by many.

---

4   John F. Helliwell, et al. "World Happiness Report 2021," Sustainable Development Solutions Network, 18.

MASLOW'S HIERARCHY OF NEEDS

Maybe you're familiar with Maslow's Hierarchy of Needs, the psychological theory that forms a pyramid, starting with physiological needs at the base and then ending with self-actualization at the top, an enlightened state in which the individual continually desires to become the best version of themselves.

As we look deeper into the factors of P-GDP in Part II and the factors of P-HI in Part III, I want to adapt this theory in what I'll conveniently call "**Vizzoca's Hierarchy of Needs**":

PERSONAL GROSS DOMESTIC PRODUCT (P-GDP) HIERARCHY

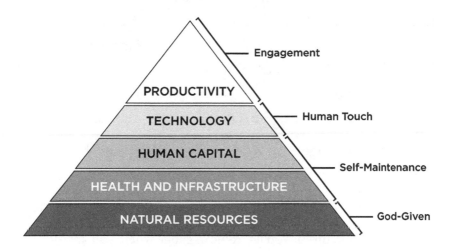

PERSONAL HAPPINESS INDEX (P-HI) HIERARCHY

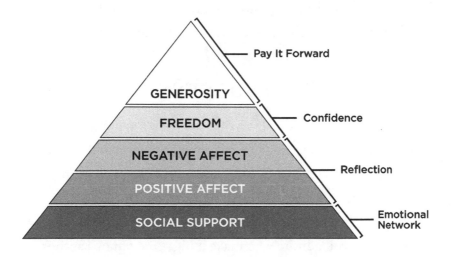

As we dive into each concept, I hope these will help you process how it all fits together and give you a framework to help guide you in the self-evaluation pieces that we'll get into in each chapter.

In each section, you will rate yourself based on the above factors that contribute to P-GDP and P-HI on a scale from +2 ("I'm doing great at this") to -2 ("Not doing so well/I don't care about this"). From those scores, you will put together a measure for both P-GDP and P-HI that will place you into "buckets" of development. Given my love for baseball, I've decided to base these buckets on the levels used in professional baseball:

- **Instructional League** (Learning phase, addressing gaps)

- **Minor League** (Developing higher skills, but there's room for improvement)

- **Major League** (You're a pro, and others want to be like you)

With this in mind, you'll be able to gauge where you are today to get a clearer view of where you need to be on your leadership journey. After all, it's not just about making it to the Major Leagues, but sustaining your place in it, making it to a championship team, attaining MVP status, and then inspiring and giving back to others along the way. No matter where you land, every day is a new chance to lead.

THE STAIRS TO SUCCESS

Honestly, I learned all this the hard way. I was the guy who thought there was a fast track to leadership. I thought I could find an elevator, punch the button labeled "CEO," and head straight to the top floor and the corner office with the great view looking down on those below me. There's no such thing as an overnight success in life. Those people you admire who make it big—the famous author, the first draft pick, the tech entrepreneur—you're seeing the end result; you're not seeing the years of hard work, practice, and mistakes they've made along the way.

The elevator to leadership doesn't exist any more than a cancer diagnosis leading straight to a cure the next day or an immigrant arriving one day and finding prosperity the same week. The only way to forgo any illusion of an elevator to success is to discover that you have to take the stairs and—you guessed it—choosing your hard. You can choose the hard that leads you to finding happiness and success, or you can choose the hard that settles for mediocrity and dissatisfaction. It's the difference between *leadership* and *leadershi**.

If you choose the hard of climbing the stairs, you *will* get tired and be faced with obstacles, your legs will feel like mush, you might stumble and fall and maybe scrape your knee, and maybe you have to stop for a bit to wait for another group to pass by the opposite direction.

You may lose a job or two along the way, but the key is to get up and keep moving forward. Each step represents an event, an experience that shapes you and creates character that will allow you to appreciate your journey and the challenges you faced to get to the next level. You may encounter others on your long journey up the stairs who give you the opportunity to travel along for a while and learn from them.

Instead of focusing on the pain of the journey up, you have to zoom in on what those experiences are teaching you. But every so often, you should stop and take a look back at how far you've come. Take a breather; stop and reflect on what you have learned so far that makes you a stronger, more well-rounded leader.

Sometimes on the stairs, you'll find a new floor of the building you didn't even know about, and you'll learn something new about yourself. Unlike an elevator, the stairs provide you the opportunity to look back and see others climbing up where you once traveled. Instead of being a jerk and saying, "Glad that's not me anymore," you have the opportunity to be a servant and extend a hand to help them up. No one gets to the top of the stairs alone—someone above you has helped guide and support you, so help someone else by being generous with whatever wisdom has helped you get where you are.

Now, to take this back to your Personal GDP and your Personal Happiness Index—if you don't have an understanding of who you are, your strengths, what makes you happy in your work, your climb up the stairs is going to be harder than it has to be. You might get off at the wrong floor because you've got the wrong destination in mind. Don't worry—you won't be the first to make that mistake—and you can always get headed back in the right direction on the stairs, but it will take longer.

One of my favorite singers of all time is country artist Garth Brooks. I've had the good fortune to see him live three times over the years, but more than his music, I admire his approach to his craft and his passion. His story took many twists and turns, but he found his strengths, his ability to sing and entertain crowds, and then he built off his strengths to persevere on his journey.

In fact, the lyrics to his song "The River" sum up the personal challenges he faced on his journey. He cowrote the song with song-writer Victoria Shaw, and in an interview with *American Songwriter* in November of 2019, Shaw spoke about the inspiration behind the song:

> That song summed up exactly what Garth and I were feeling. We both wanted success so badly, though I have to say, he saw it even clearer than I did. He *knew* he was going to play arenas someday. I just thought he was delusional because nobody had done that in country music and it seemed way too ambitious. Ha! A few years later I had the pleasure of being Garth's opening act at his historic Central Park concert where I got to witness one million fans waving their lighters and singing *our* song![5]

---

5   Doug Waterman, "The Story Behind the Song: Victoria Shaw & Garth Brooks, 'The River,'" *American Songwriter*, November 2019.

Whether it's a change in your dreams, life, career, or circumstances, you may fall, but you need to stay focused on the reward. Garth Brooks has obviously taken this advice and has found both success and happiness, but, more importantly, he has looked back from the top of the stairs to help others climb up, giving back through his generosity.

In my eyes, no journey is "perfect," but the ability to look at yourself, evaluate your strengths, and recognize your weaknesses is significant. After all, you can't *always* stop adversity from coming your way—you can't always stop the you-know-what from hitting the fan, but those imperfect situations give you the chance to grow and become a better person and, ultimately, a better leader. Combining those opportunities with understanding your true happiness makes you a leader. Not everyone has the fortitude to be honest with themselves and do the hard work and introspection it requires. But I promise it'll be worth it.

> **No journey is "perfect," but the ability to look at yourself, evaluate your strengths, and recognize your weaknesses is significant.**

In Part II, we're going to dig deeper into each factor of Personal GDP so that you can get a clearer understanding of what that looks like for you. In Part III, we'll deep dive into the Personal Happiness Index to help you discover where your passions and satisfaction lie so you can be more confident you're climbing the right stairway.

At one point, I thought about calling this book *Mom, Where Do Leaders Come From?* So consider this "the talk," all about how when P-GDP and P-HI get together—boom—it makes a leader. My hope is that the marriage of these two measures will absolutely transform not only how you measure yourself as a leader, but also how you measure success in your team and your organization, as well as, hopefully, how you inspire it in those around you for an impact that will outlive you.

PART 2
PERSONAL GDP

CHAPTER 2
NATURAL RESOURCES

Any time you have an opportunity to make a difference in this world and you don't, then you are wasting your time on Earth.
— *ROBERTO CLEMENTE*

No one gets to pick their natural resources in life—their strengths, their talents, the ways they process information. If so, we'd all be first-round drafts for insert-sport-of-your-choice. And no one gets to pick the challenges they face either. But here's the thing about challenges: they have a way of making us choose our hard and helping us really see what our natural resources are.

Every school has that kid who is insanely talented and just seems like they have it all. In my high school, it definitely wasn't me. No, that was John Siciliano. I can still remember him knocking it out of the park as the Cowardly Lion in our school's production of *The Wizard of Oz*. And speaking of knocking it out of the park, he was also a star baseball and soccer player. There were no doubts he was going to make it big.

Until life threw him a giant curveball. In June of 1993, on the way to celebrate the end of a successful semester at college, he was in a car wreck and had to have his leg amputated above the knee. I still remember going to see him a couple days after he'd been admitted to the hospital and feeling devastated. What do you say to the guy who just had his dreams taken away from him?

Thank God that wasn't how John saw it. He realized pretty quickly that losing a leg didn't make him lose his love of acting or athletics. If anything, it just gave him new motivation, new drive, and newfound courage to pursue his dreams—no matter what.

And that's just what he did. In 1996, he represented the US in the Paralympic Games in Atlanta. In 2002, he got his first role on a popular award-winning television show, which opened the door for more roles onstage, on TV, and in film. He found that there were roles available that only someone like him could play.

He may have lost one type of natural resource—his leg—but found success by utilizing the other natural resources that had always been there: courage, perseverance, resiliency, and passion. On top of his work in entertainment, he also goes around to schools as a public speaker, encouraging students everywhere to pursue their dreams and find courage in the face of challenges. Does John wish he still had his leg? I'm sure he does. But as I've watched him from afar, it seems to me like losing his leg has also given him unique opportunities to touch lives and make an impact that may have never happened otherwise.

Now, John's story may seem a bit more dramatic than what most of us will face. But it illustrates one of the most valuable things I think any leader can learn: challenges can reveal strength. While you don't get to choose the challenges in life, you can choose your hard in how you face it—you can choose to run from it and risk missing out on the reward, or you can choose to overcome it. It's in overcoming the challenge that we find our greatness.

PERSONAL NATURAL RESOURCES

In the last chapter, I talked about how the first factor of P-GDP is exactly the same as GDP: natural resources. Every nation, no matter their size or history, has natural resources available to them, and it's no different with people. One of the most harmful things you can do in your leadership journey is start comparing yourself to others and fall into the trap of thinking you need to have exactly the same resources as someone else. Maybe you're not a Mark Zuckerberg, you're not a Bill Gates—so what? The world already has enough of them.

Instead, this is about identifying your natural resources instead of sitting around wishing you had someone else's. I could be wrong, but I don't think Saudi Arabia sits around saying, "Man, I wish we had more iron ore like Australia." No—they keep pumping petroleum out of the ground and then sell it to Australia.

Likewise, as an individual, you've got to understand and appreciate what you have available to you—the things that make you great—rather than focus on what you don't have. The longer you stay stuck on your perceived weaknesses, the longer you let those weaknesses rule over you instead of building up your strengths and using them.

The key is to be grateful for what you *do* have. Okay, so you're not a Hall of Famer. Guess what? I'm not one either. But if you've got two working eyes, two working ears, working legs and arms, then you've got a lot to be grateful for. Too often, we take those things for granted until they get taken away from us.

There's a lot of people out there who have natural abilities that aren't getting exercised because they're too focused on the ones they don't have. Not only are they missing out on using

> The longer you stay stuck on your perceived weaknesses, the longer you let those weaknesses rule over you.

their God-given abilities, but they're missing out on the chance to make a difference in the world.

Self-doubt is one of the greatest obstacles any of us will have to face when identifying our natural resources. You might think, "I'm just a parking attendant, I'm just a receptionist," or whatever you want to fill in the blank with. It can be tempting to let your job title define you instead of letting your strengths do that.

So instead of looking just at what you do every day, a natural starting point is to look at what you're interested in. Like I mentioned before, I always wanted to work in healthcare, and realizing I didn't have the natural strengths to be a doctor wasn't going to stop me from finding a way into the field. If I'd let self-doubt rule the day, who knows where I would've ended up or what I would've settled for.

TANGIBLE AND INTANGIBLE

A big difference between GDP and P-GDP is how those resources show themselves. With GDP, a nation's resources are typically tangible goods, but with P-GDP, your natural resources could be a tangible quality—like physical strength or a talent—or an intangible quality like resiliency, empathy, and determination. The point is, you need to know how to identify both your tangible *and* intangible resources.

This goes back to why I'm always looking for people with the Spirit of the Immigrant. Immigrants by necessity have to be able to identify their natural resources of both types and put them to use to find success in their new country. My mother was a seamstress from a young age, so by the time she came to America, she could make you just about anything you could ask for: three-piece suits, dresses, drapes … you name it. So for her, it was about putting that tangible resource to good use both for our family and to make herself indispensable to the community.

With my dad, it was more about those intangible resources—his drive and determination to make sure our family was taken care of and to see his kids have better opportunities than he'd had. When he first came to America, he was making $1.75 an hour working for a greeting card company, which was good money compared to what he could've done in Italy. But when the company talked about relocating, he had to come up with another plan. That's when he heard about the opportunity to become a port authority bus driver, which meant he could make $13 or $14 an hour. The only problem was that he didn't exactly have the qualifications for the job.

But out of sheer determination, he wasn't going to let anything stand in his way of an opportunity like that, knowing the difference that could make for all of us. Not only did he get the job, but in his twenty-five years of driving, he didn't have a single incident—not just because he ended up being a great driver but because he was determined to do the best job he could for our sake. I like to think that I inherited that intangible resource of drive from him.

Everyone's got both tangible and intangible resources. It's just a matter of figuring out what they are so you can put them to use. While there are various strength-finding tools and tests out there, like Gallup's Clifton Strengths assessment, I want to help you think a little bit outside of the box.

EXERCISE: WORK LINEAGE

You've probably heard of DNA and heritage-tracing tools like 23andMe or Ancestry.com. Until I took one of those tests myself, I always thought I was 100 percent Italian, only to find out that I was 69 percent Italian with some Greek and Turkish thrown into the mix. It helped me realize there was a bigger story behind how I got here than just what was obvious.

No matter who you are, I think there's a natural curiosity to find out where you come from. What's funny to me is that we do that with our biological lineage, but we never think to do the same with our **Work Lineage**.

If you're struggling to figure out what your natural resources are, I've found this to be a powerful exercise to start figuring it out. Draw out a Work Lineage for yourself. What did your parents do? Then your grandparents? And your great-grandparents, if you can find that out. Beyond just what they did for work, though, you have to look at their personalities, their skills. Once you start mapping that out, you're going to start seeing some patterns and some overlaps with yourself. In fact, you might start to find out some things about yourself you never knew.

Now, that doesn't mean you have to be pigeonholed into doing the same thing the generations before you did. It would be like if I had decided that, because I'm Italian, I had to be really good at making wine or sausage. That's just falling into a stereotype, not actually looking at your lineage.

Take my friend Kelly—every woman in her family has gotten a degree in education and been a schoolteacher. Everyone expected she would do the same. But that's not what she wanted to do. Instead, she wanted to run her own business, so she went to school to learn business. Now she runs a successful marketing company where—guess what—she gets to educate people on how to best promote and grow their businesses.

Also, your Work Lineage doesn't just have to be your family. Maybe you have no clue what your family's Work Lineage is. I think then you have to start mapping out who the most influential people in your life have been—mentors, coaches, teachers, or leaders that you've followed. And you start looking at their strengths, what you admire about them and how that's impacted you.

So take out a piece of paper and start mapping it out. What made your influencers unique and where did they find any success? Which of those qualities do you see in yourself? Did you inherit a tangible talent or skill from your influencers? Or do you see a pattern of intangible resources that have been passed down to you from family or mentors?

EXERCISE: SELF EXIT INTERVIEW

Maybe you've had to fill out an exit interview when leaving a job. What I've always found interesting—and even frustrating—about these is that they usually ask questions that might actually be more helpful when you're *starting* a new job or project. But that's a whole other rant for another book.

In this exercise, you have to imagine that you're leaving your current job and ask yourself the following questions:

- Did you feel like the organization valued you and your abilities?

- Did the organization provide you with tools and opportunities to grow your strengths?

- What qualities should the organization look for in your replacement?

- If you could change one thing about the job you had, what would it be and why?

- What do you feel was your greatest contribution to the organization?

Because you're probably not used to asking yourself these questions every day, a few things should stand out. First, most of us have a tendency to overemphasize our faults, so this should help you see what you value in yourself, and by extension, what others should value about you. Ideally, this should be a list of both tangible and intangible resources.

Second, it should help you isolate what you do best and assess whether you are actively growing those natural resources. If you're not taking the opportunities to grow in your strengths, then you're not fully appreciating them. Remember, even the greatest athletes need to eat well, sleep well, and train hard to maximize their God-given gifts.

Third, it should give you some motivation to take a hard look at what you're doing *now* and figure out whether it's what you *should* be doing. I think most of us have ended up in jobs that turned out different than what we expected or hoped for. Sometimes that's what it takes to figure out where your natural resources would be best put to use to make a difference in the world.

SELF-ASSESSMENT

Moment of truth. It's time to measure yourself in terms of your Natural Resources. Now, here's the deal—I can't force you to be honest with yourself. Only you can do that. So just keep in mind that there's not much of a point to this exercise if you're not willing to show some honest introspection as you measure yourself.

Get used to it now because you're going to be ranking yourself on each factor, and at the end of the book, we're going to put together all your scores so you can see how you measure up on your leadership journey—where you're doing well and where you need work as you grow your P-GDP. We'll be using a modified version of the Likert scale where 2 is the highest level of agreement and -2 is the lowest level of agreement.

	1. I CAN EASILY IDENTIFY MY NATURAL RESOURCES.
2	I can easily identify my natural resources, and I actively look for ways to put them to use.
1	I can identify some of my natural resources but don't actively use them all.
0	I know I have natural resources, but I don't give them much thought.
-1	I don't think about my natural resources unless someone else points them out.
-2	I've never thought about my natural resources or how to use them.

Now, regardless of where you just scored yourself, take some time to think about what your natural resources might be. Open your notes app on your phone or jot them down in a journal. Wherever you write them down, just make sure it's somewhere you will be forced to *see* and *think* about them.

	2. I UNDERSTAND AND RECOGNIZE THE ORIGINS OF MY NATURAL RESOURCES.
2	I can identify the origins of most of my natural resources.
1	I have some idea of the origins of some of my natural resources.
0	I've never thought much about the origins of my natural resources.
-1	I only think about the origins of my natural resources when others bring it up.
-2	I struggle to think about where my natural resources come from.

Again, regardless of the number you just selected, you should take some time to do the exercise I mentioned above about your Work

Lineage. What were the strengths of your parents? Your grandparents? Other influential individuals in your life? What talents have been passed down? What patterns emerge?

3. I AM UTILIZING MY NATURAL RESOURCES TO THEIR FULLEST POTENTIAL IN MY CURRENT ROLE.	
2	Not only am I utilizing my natural resources to their fullest potential in my role, but I'm also growing them.
1	I am utilizing a lot of my natural resources in my current role.
0	I'm utilizing some of my natural resources in my role but not with any consistency.
-1	I'm not utilizing many of my natural resources in my current role.
-2	None of my natural resources are being used in my current role.

4. MY ORGANIZATION RECOGNIZES MY NATURAL RESOURCES AND PLACES ME IN SITUATIONS TO UTILIZE THEM.	
2	My organization recognizes my natural resources and consistently places me in a position to maximize my natural resources and grow them.
1	My organization recognizes most of my natural resources and gives me some opportunity to put them to use.
0	My organization may be aware of my natural resources but does not consistently put me in a position to utilize them.
-1	I don't know if my organization recognizes my natural resources or cares how I put them to use.
-2	My organization couldn't care less about my natural resources or how I use them.

Now, I want you to think about both of these questions side by side for a second. I know we can't live in a perfect world where everyone has the perfect job at the perfect place designed specifically for them, but if you're going to maximize your potential as a leader, you have to honestly ask if the role you are in uses your gifts to the fullest. Take a few minutes to do the Self Exit Interview and assess how your current role and organization helps you utilize—or fails to help you utilize—your natural resources.

5. MY SUPERVISOR WANTS MY NATURAL RESOURCES TO BENEFIT ME AS MUCH AS THEY BENEFIT THE ORGANIZATION/SUPERVISOR.	
2	My supervisor is adamant about helping me grow my natural resources for my own self-improvement and benefit, knowing this will also benefit the organization.
1	My supervisor occasionally looks for ways to help me grow my natural resources for my own self-improvement and benefit.
0	My supervisor encourages some growth in my natural resources but mostly in regards to how it benefits the organization. If it also benefits me personally, it's an unintended bonus.
-1	My supervisor only encourages my growth if it benefits their position or the organization.
-2	All my supervisor is concerned about is having a warm body to get a job done.

Speaking from experience, even if you're the CEO, there is someone you answer to in your organization. As a leader, you're constantly pouring into others—or you should be—and it's no different with whoever is leading you. Are they pouring into you? And if so, how often and why? Is it just to check something off their list to make themselves look good, or do they truly value you?

Take a few moments to think of some examples of how your supervisor has given you the opportunity to utilize your talents and skills for your benefit and not just to help themselves. And if you can't think of any examples, then make a list of some ways that you would like for your supervisor to help you better use and grow your natural resources.

CONCLUSION

Does your brain hurt yet? Then maybe take a minute to grab a drink (no judgments here on what kind) and take some deep breaths. And then once you get back, add up the scores above to get your overall Natural Resources score.

No matter what you scored—high or low—I've got news for you. If you didn't score as high as you hoped, the good news is that you can grow and improve, and now you've got some ideas of how that can happen. At the very least, you should have a good list to build off of and some good ideas on how to move forward.

So whether you are going to work on improving the score you got—or work on maintaining it— knowing your natural resources is just the first step in how you manage the hard things life will throw at you.

If you scored high, the news is that you don't get to just sit back in the shade and coast. Success oftentimes leads to complacency and complacency to mediocrity. In P-GDP, having one strong measurement does not necessarily ensure personal success. It's about having balance between the factors. Think of them like the legs of a relay race—it's not the team with the fastest individual runner that wins but the team with the most consistently fast runners.

So whether you are going to work on improving the score you got—or work on maintaining it—knowing your natural resources is just the first step in how you manage the hard things life will throw at you. It's like knowing who's on your team roster, but you've still got to make a game plan, practice, and play the game—which is why you've got to see if you have a healthy environment and the right infrastructure in place to set those natural resources into motion.

CHAPTER 3

HEALTH AND INFRASTRUCTURE

They always say time changes things, but you
actually have to change them yourself.
— *ANDY WARHOL*

It's cliché to say that the only constant in life is change. You probably don't need me to tell you that. But the way I see it, there are two main types of changes: external changes—the ones that happen to you—and internal changes—the ones you choose to make.

In 2016, I needed to make a change in a big way. I'd spent fifteen years in various roles at the same large health system, and I found myself getting burned out quickly. I knew my routine day to day—that wasn't the issue. But somewhere along the way, I seemed to have lost the *why* of what I was doing and, more importantly, *who* I was doing it for.

Ever been there? If so, welcome to **Club Burnout**.

One time, a staff member gifted me a book; on the inside cover, he wrote me a note sharing some incredible wisdom: *People get burned out not because of the work they do but because they forget why we do it.*

That was me. As much as this burnout was affecting my professional health, it was also having a profound impact on my mental and physical health. The constant work and stress were causing me to neglect exercise, spend less time with my family, and I even found myself suffering from anxiety attacks and heart palpitations to the point of waking up in the middle of the night more times than I care to admit.

Old habits die hard, though, don't they? Even after becoming CEO at my new job, fifteen years of nonstop, high-pressure work had conditioned me to operate in a constant state of overdrive. In fact, I almost passed out after my first public appearance during a golf tournament fundraiser. The worst part is I didn't even play in the tournament where I might have the excuse—I was just *that* worn down.

But the real wake-up call was when I went in for an orthopedic appointment for some knee pain and discovered I was the heaviest I'd ever been. Point blank: I needed to take better care of myself.

Real change provokes action, so my wife and I joined Weight Watchers right away. Now, before I get in trouble, let me clarify: she didn't need to lose any weight herself, but she was there to give me moral support and accountability. After six months, my health transformed as I lost sixty pounds, the anxiety attacks disappeared, and the heart palpitations reduced. And as a gift for my wife's support, I stopped snoring.

On top of these physical and mental improvements, I also found a renewed energy and focus in my work and leadership. I didn't know it then, but all of these internal changes were helping me prepare for the greatest external change—and greatest professional challenge—that I would face in light of the COVID-19 health crisis. But more on that soon.

HEALTH AND INFRASTRUCTURE (OR LACK THEREOF)

We tend to try to segment the different parts of our life like one doesn't affect the other, but life is more holistic than that. When I went in for that appointment for my knee, it wasn't really just about my knee, was it? My mental health affected my physical health—and vice-versa.

When a nation is focusing on their health systems and infrastructure, it's always about how those two elements affect the *whole* country. In the end, it's all about looking ahead to the future, because while you can't control what external changes come along, you can implement *internal* changes.

> In the end, it's all about looking ahead to the future, because while you can't control what external changes come along, you can implement internal changes.

On the surface, Health and Infrastructure might not seem to go hand in hand, but they couldn't be more related. But countries that are serious about improving their GDP ask, "How can we better move goods across the country for economic health? How can we ensure proper medical care to our citizens to avoid a health crisis?"

And it should be the same with your Personal Health and Infrastructure (or lack thereof):

HEALTH: What is the state of your body, mind, and spirit?

INFRASTRUCTURE: What tools and resources do you have in place to improve and maintain the state of your health?

Whether it's a personal or professional change that needs to be made, measuring your Personal GDP means taking a hard, honest look at the different aspects of your health, seeing how they relate to each other, and finding the ways to improve them.

This is not a one and done exercise but a lifetime commitment to taking care of yourself. No matter what you do as a leader, you're either working to improve the health of your Mind, Body, and Spirit—or working to maintain it. Both require you to have the proper infrastructure to make that possible.

HEALTH: BODY, MIND, AND SPIRIT

If you don't know where to start, that's normal. This is a judgment-free zone. To help you brainstorm, here are some of the activities I do to invest in each area of my health:

Body: I really enjoy running and walking, which I've found helps me release stress from my body and clear my mind. I prefer doing this after work but before family time so I'm not dumping all my stress on them.

Now, maybe running isn't your exercise of choice. Maybe it's golf or biking. Or axe-throwing. But whatever you choose, it needs to be something you'll enjoy and that you'll be able to make time for consistently without totally reinventing your schedule.

Mind: I like to engage my mind with learning and improve my concentration through listening to podcasts, meditation, and stretching. You might prefer reading, or puzzles, or watching documentaries. The key is to pick an activity that will keep your mind active and alert.

Spirit: For me, this is easy—I pray ... a lot. Working for a faith-based organization, I've learned from the Sisters that instead of worrying about a decision, I should pray about it, and then the decision will come to me. In fact, I've adopted a mantra instilled in me by the Sisters: "Pray (or in some cases meditate) on it."

Now, I know not everyone is religious, so maybe prayer isn't your thing. Maybe it's donating your time to a charitable cause or playing music—whatever gets you in touch with your spirit to find balance and see the bigger picture in your life. To me, seeing the bigger picture means you have a set of beliefs that keep you grounded and help you find balance in work and life so that you can approach each day with focus, calm, and strength.

You've probably noticed there is overlap between these areas. While running benefits my physical health, it also helps my mental health. Likewise, when I do stretching for my mental health, it's engaging my body. When you're pursuing health in one area, it's natural for it to benefit your health in other areas. Two birds, one stone.

As a rule of thumb, I think it's good to look for these overlaps and pursue those activities. Instead of piling on activities to check off the boxes, it's about efficiency and simplification. In other words, unpack your psyche—and only pack what you need.

INFRASTRUCTURE: SOFT, HARD, AND CRITICAL

Maybe you're familiar with the phrase "Leaders Eat Last." I agree that's true, but in order for you to thrive as a leader, you need to have the mental and physical energy to see that you must not only be willing to eat last, but that you may be the one to set the table, gather the ingredients, or even cook the meal!

With GDP, infrastructure is always broken down into Soft, Hard, and Critical areas. Within P-GDP, we'll do exactly the same thing, linking those three areas back to the health of your Mind, Body, and Spirit.

SOFT INFRASTRUCTURE (SPIRIT)

GDP describes Soft Infrastructure as that which is supportive in nature by maintaining the economy through areas such as government systems, law enforcement, and education. These areas instill confidence and support for citizens within society. The term "soft" refers to the fact that these areas are less tangible and more behind the scenes in their function.

Within P-GDP, Soft Infrastructure refers to the Spirit or the culture that drives a person, team, or organization. As a leader, this Spirit is the philosophy and culture *you* create through your actions, driven by your values. Because it's more intangible, the Spirit is not always going to show up in a board report, but rather it's something that is felt through actions—specifically *your* actions. If you value support and innovation, creativity and passion—it has to show in you first before it'll show up in your team.

Whether you realize it or not, you bring a spirit to work every day, and you have the choice of whether it's going to be one that encourages freedom and support—or one of entitled superiority, aka "my way or the highway" thinking—or what we call "egonomics."

Remember, it's the *big picture* you bring that will determine the balance—or imbalance—of the organization. In my opinion, there is nothing more detrimental to a leader, team, or organization than a culture that is stifling, demoralizing, or restraining.

HARD INFRASTRUCTURE (BODY)

GDP describes Hard infrastructure as those components which are outwardly visible, tangible, easily assessed and monitored for necessary maintenance. This would represent highways, bridges, and roads as well as the various modes of transportation needed, like buses, trains, cars, ferries, and so on.

The Hard infrastructure within P-GDP directly correlates to your Body, or physical health. As a leader, the most important thing you can do is take care of yourself in order to handle the rigors of leading. It asks: "Hey, are you prepared for the physical and mental stressors that come with being responsible for the lives of others?"

But you don't stop there. Professionally speaking, it also asks: "What tools are you going to provide to take care of your team—the people that work to take care of you?" Because if you do all the prep work for the meal and don't provide some eating utensils, then everyone's going to have a hard time eating. And where's the fun in that?

CRITICAL INFRASTRUCTURE (MIND)

In a functioning society, there are structures in place to regulate and oversee various areas. This is what GDP would define as Critical Infrastructure. Another way to think about it is as those components that lead to direct action. For example, in the United States, we have agencies such as Homeland Security, the Department of Energy, the Department of Transportation, and so on.

Within P-GDP, we would refer to this as the Mind, or the area where we do the thinking and planning to bring clarity and reduce ambiguity for ourselves and our teams. No matter what kind of organization you're in, there are governing bodies that make the rules and regulations you follow, but you also need your own policies and procedures in place to help you get in the right frame of mind to conduct your business.

Jack Nicklaus, arguably the greatest golfer of all time, once said, "I never hit a shot, not even in practice, without having a very sharp, in-focus picture of it in my head." In other words, his thoughts led directly to action. Likewise, I tell my kids all the time, "Think differently, then make it happen."

PREPARED

It's worth saying again: real change provokes action. I didn't realize back in 2016 when I decided to take better care of my health how the internal changes I chose would help me and my team prepare for the greatest external change—and crisis—we have had to face.

> **It's worth saying again: real change provokes action.**

After reaping the personal benefits of getting my body, mind, and spirit back to a good place, I decided to start up a voluntary wellness program. This included identifying spaces in our facilities that could be converted into gyms for the employees instead of them having to pay for expensive gym memberships.

But we also started providing nutritional seminars (lunch and learns), biometric screening events, financial wellness resources, and mental wellness resources. I wanted there to be an infrastructure in place for us to encourage and enable health for our employees on every level—especially as a healthcare organization! Every year we see more and more participants and hear feedback on how these resources are making a tangible impact in their personal *and* professional lives.

In November 2019, we pledged to raise our minimum wage to $15 an hour. Keep in mind—we're a nonprofit, but we wanted to literally put our money where our mouth was and show our staff that they are our greatest asset. That same month, we approved the creation of a clinical excellence team to serve as a conduit to respond to external organizations, including medical institutions and government agencies.

All of these plans and purposeful changes were put in place out of a desire to be innovative and make sure we had the internal health and infrastructure to face whatever external change might come our way.

And boy, did it come.

On December 1, 2019, the World Health Organization (WHO) announced the first known case of COVID-19. On January 1, 2020, we went ahead and announced our new clinical excellence team so we could discuss how we would face this challenge with our existing infrastructure. How would we handle an outbreak in a facility? Where were our gaps in terms of personnel, facility, and procedures?

Twenty days later, we got the news no one wanted: there was an outbreak at a senior care facility in the state of Washington. This was it. We had to move quickly—and we did. From day one, I made one thing abundantly clear to our team: in times of crisis, the true leaders would rise to the occasion, and I would make swift decisions on those who were not up to the task.

Reflecting back, I can correlate each step to the same P-GDP Infrastructure concept:

Soft (Spirit and Culture)—While I knew we already had a supportive culture that would encourage a sense of calm and focus, I knew I had to reinforce my own sense of confidence as an example to my team. What was about to happen was not normal … far from it. So you better believe I increased my prayer time to prepare my spirit for it.

Hard (Body, Physical Health)—I also needed people to understand that as we prepared, we would have long days and evenings that would take a toll on our mental and physical health. So I needed everyone to take care of themselves, to do the best we could to prevent burnout and maintain our own health while interacting with patients.

I closely monitored behavior among the staff and made certain to give rest and praise frequently because we all needed to be strong. With the employee wellness program already firmly established, I fully believe that our staff was starting out in a better physical and mental condition than other organizations.

For myself, I started setting an alarm to remind myself to go on twenty-minute walks during the day and eat small meals to keep my metabolism and mood up. No one needs a "hangry" leader.

But we also needed an infrastructure to care for patients. I needed the bridges and roads, if you will. While this included stocking up on PPE equipment, we also contacted one of our partner construction firms and explained we needed to construct a negative air pressure isolation unit within our existing facility—and we needed it in six weeks.

You can imagine the reaction from the contractor … And, by the way, we also needed to recruit new staff specifically to care for infected patients. It was a lot of work, but in late February of 2020, our two isolation COVID units were ready and staffed as we waited for whatever might come next.

Critical (Mind Policies, Procedures, Regulations … Thought)—While the pandemic raged and was in full swing, the reality was that we still needed to operate within the rules and regulations that the federal government and CMS (Centers for Medicaid and Medicare Services) and state DOH (Department of Health) had already set forth.

Meanwhile, our new clinical excellence team was busy creating our own procedures and processes specifically to address the pandemic. Operating with a purpose that I had never seen in my three years there, we knew what we had to do and how to do it, but more importantly, our minds were primed to be innovative and imaginative.

We became an example and shared our processes with not only government agencies, but also with our competitors because lives were on the line, and I'll never apologize for saving a life.

For myself, I was increasing my meditation time to thirty-minute sessions to bring myself to a place of clarity and creativity. This allowed me to give my team and myself the freedom to think differently, without ridicule or fear.

Throughout the crisis, I had one rule for myself and my team: think quickly and act quicker. Having the right mindset and policies provided the guide rails to keep us centered on quality and ethics in every hard decision. We were able to do this because I believed we had a team with the health and infrastructure to take calculated risks. Sometimes you might make a wrong decision—yes—but the key is to be prepared for either outcome of the action you decide to take. After all, failing doesn't make you a failure—giving up does.

SELF-ASSESSMENT

But enough about me. What about you? How do you measure up in your Personal Health and Infrastructure?

No offense if you're a fan of them, but I personally hate DISC assessments. I think it's too easy to lie to yourself by projecting your ideal self into the results. But starting your leadership journey by lying to yourself is going to lead to being an artificial leader. You only hurt yourself when you do that—and it could lead to hurting your team in the long run.

Instead, I'd encourage you to do a self-inspection. Just like how the leaders of nations do a state of the union, you should do a state of the *you*-nion (pun very much intended). Doing this helps you become *preventative* rather than *reactive*. It's difficult to revoke your membership to Club Burnout, but it can be done through making the right Personal Infrastructure changes that will improve your Physical, Mental, and Spiritual Health.

MY PHYSICAL HEALTH NEVER INTERFERES WITH MY CAPABILITIES.	
2	I listen to my body. I am in a healthy state to give my all to my family and work, including doing an annual state of the you-nion.
1	I am in overall good physical health, but there are areas of improvement I need to take, and I need to be more proactive.
0	I am in okay health, but I am making excuses for not pursuing better health.
-1	I realize I am not in good health and know I need to improve but have not yet taken any steps or put any thought into making improvements.
-2	My physical health is clearly contributing to a loss of productivity and negatively impacting my focus, leadership abilities, and relationships.

No matter where you are on this scale, the good news is that you can start taking actions *today* to change your trajectory! Excuses lead the way on the path to mediocrity. Again, you get to choose your hard—obtaining a healthy BMI is hard, but so is hypertension and heart disease.

2. MENTAL HEALTH: MY MIND IS ALWAYS FOCUSED, AND I HAVE COMPLETE CONTROL OVER IT.	
2	I am able to clear my mind prior to falling asleep, and I have techniques and a routine in place to help maintain focus during the day.
1	I am not always focused, and I worry at times, but I have techniques and tools to help get me back on track pretty quickly.
0	I get distracted by worries on a weekly basis, but I am aware of ways I can start addressing these.
-1	Worries and stress affect me on a daily basis, and I am unsure of how to start addressing those issues.
-2	Worries and stress consume most of my day, I am unable to still my mind at night, and I don't know where to begin to regain focus.

There is no shame in admitting you need help with your mental health. According to National Institute of Mental Health data, one in five adults in the US are living with some form of mental illness, including anxiety. Don't put off addressing it; ignoring it only makes it worse.

	3. SPIRITUAL HEALTH: MY BELIEFS ALLOW ME TO ALWAYS SEE THE BIGGER PICTURE AND CREATE A CULTURE OF CALM, FOCUS, AND STRENGTH.
2	I have a consistent routine that encourages a work-life balance and a focus on the bigger picture to keep perspective on what truly matters in life.
1	I can identify my beliefs and what brings me peace, and I am able to remind myself of the bigger picture most of the time.
0	I sometimes think about my spiritual health but often lose focus on the bigger picture.
-1	I almost never think about my spiritual health, and I am not certain of how to identify my beliefs or see the bigger picture.
-2	I cannot think of the last time I felt grounded or at peace and have lost sight of the bigger picture and feel totally out of balance in my life.

Remember, spiritual health isn't exclusively about religious beliefs or practices. Someone can go to church or temple every day of their life and still be out of balance if they are not actively exercising those beliefs. If you scored on the lower end here, then take some time to make a list of your firmly held beliefs, and think about the times in your life you have felt most at peace and balanced. Use that list as your baseline and starting point! Even if you scored really well here, I'd encourage you to do the same thing to serve as a daily reminder.

4. I COLLABORATE WELL WITH OTHERS TO ACCOMPLISH GOALS AND REDUCE THE CHANCE OF BURNOUT FOR MYSELF AND OTHERS.	
2	I see teamwork as a vital form of infrastructure in my organization and actively encourage it so that the burden of work is spread evenly and the whole team can share in success.
1	I work well with others in general, but I can be inconsistent in how I encourage collaboration.
0	I have a tendency to take care of things myself instead of thinking about collaborating with a team, but I will collaborate in the right circumstances with specific individuals.
-1	I will work with others if I have to but tend to see this as a hindrance because I don't have a lot of trust in the abilities of others on the team to get the job done right.
-2	I avoid working with others at all costs because I have no faith in my team and would rather have too much on my plate than entrust others with tasks.

Maybe you're wondering how this question fits into measuring your Personal Infrastructure. As we look ahead to Human Capital, though, I think it's important to gauge whether you have the right infrastructure of *people* on your team to accomplish the work at hand. Sometimes an aversion to teamwork is rooted in not being surrounded by the right people. If your people are your most important asset, then having the right team is paramount, and teamwork will become part of the infrastructure and health of your organization.

Other times, a low score here may be rooted in your personal preference to be a "lone wolf," whether because you think you're more productive this way or because you don't like sharing credit. But the lone wolf is the least likely to survive, which is exactly why wolves live and work in packs to begin with. Teamwork is an essential infrastructure for avoiding burnout. I could never have survived the 2020 pandemic without my team—but that also meant assessing whether

I had the right team who I could collaborate with and who could collaborate with each other to get the job done.

	5. I HAVE THE TOOLS TO IMPROVE AND GROW MY PERSONAL INFRASTRUCTURE, BOTH PERSONALLY AND PROFESSIONALLY.
2	I have access to resources that will help me improve the health of my body, mind, and spirit to achieve a work-life balance and fight against burnout.
1	I have access to most of the resources that will help me improve my health, but I need to become more engaged in utilizing those resources to their full potential.
0	I have access to some of the resources that will help me improve my health, but I need to spend more time finding the right infrastructure for each area.
-1	I am only able to identify access to a few tools to improve my areas of health.
-2	Not only do I not have access to tools to improve my infrastructure, but I have no idea where to begin to look for them.

Here I'd like to reiterate the importance of conducting a state of the *you*-nion. As you identified areas of improvement, were you also able to identify resources to make the improvement happen? Because this is about work-life balance, not all of the tools or resources will come from your organization, but a good first step is to make two lists: those you have access to through your work (i.e., health insurance, PTO, etc.) and those you have access to outside your work (i.e., counselor, gym membership, social support, etc.).

CONCLUSION

While writing this book, I answered these questions for myself, and you know what? I didn't score perfectly. I found plenty of areas where I could do better and improve my areas of health despite all the progress I've made.

One thing about being a healthy leader is recognizing that doing the right thing isn't always going to make you popular. In the early days of the pandemic, I received emails, letters, and voice mails from families of our clients that were very critical of me and the plan we were enacting. Some were upset that family visitations were being restricted; others told me I was being selfish for being willing to introduce a deadly virus to a virus-free facility—and that I should be held responsible for causing any resulting outbreak.

And the criticism was coming from colleagues and competitors too. The scuttlebutt behind my back was that our plan—along with my crazy notion of paying employees a living wage—was going to bankrupt us.

While these thoughts may have entered my mind for a second, I never second-guessed what I knew was right. Despite the negativity, my only concern was keeping our residents, patients, and staff healthy, safe, and protected—and if someone did get infected, making sure that we had an environment filled with compassion to nurse them back to health.

Long story short, our foresight proved not only effective for us, but also for our entire region. We quickly became the go-to organization for large healthcare providers and other senior care facilities who had outbreaks and needed help. Suddenly, the COVID units that were once thought of as crazy became an innovative and genius lifeline.

Oh—and the families that were criticizing me? Well, they were suddenly grateful that their family members were given the best environment possible to recover. During the time those units were open, we cared for hundreds of patients, many of whom recovered and were able to go home or return to their original care facilities.

When faced with challenges and resistance, it's easy to slip back into bad habits, so I needed constant reality checks throughout the crisis. I had to revisit my health needs daily and refocus on my own infrastructure. I made the decision early on that I wouldn't settle for mediocrity anymore, in myself or others. Just like how I had to cut down my weight to become healthier, I decided during the pandemic that the bottom 5 percent of performers would have to go to keep up the health of the company. Was that easy? Hell no. But that was the hard I chose.

As Winston Churchill once said, "Never let a good crisis go to waste." For me, this included eliminating a critical role in the company during the earliest days of the pandemic. This seemed insane—believe me, it *felt* insane. But I was entrusted with the lives of both employees and residents, and I needed to do what was best for them, including making internal changes to the human capital of our team.

When implementing changes in your health and infrastructure, it's important to always be asking, "What have I learned about myself from this?" You choose your hard, and you keep looking forward.

CHAPTER 4

HUMAN CAPITAL

The saddest thing in life is wasted talent.
— *CHAZZ PALMINTERI* (A BRONX TALE)

Organizations focus on profits, revenue, and strategy, but their focus should be on their biggest capital asset: their people. It's one thing to say your people are your biggest asset—it's a whole other thing to actually show it. In my opinion, you can't find your talent without finding it in others too. To put together a kick-ass team, you've gotta be a kick-asset leader.

A few years ago, we started our employee recognition program, in which we would give any worker aspiring to move into leadership positions the opportunity to do exactly that by undergoing a rigorous process to learn every aspect of the organization, rotating through finance, operations, even shadowing me to better understand the big picture of the entire organization and learn from other leaders.

We have had an overwhelmingly positive response. One of the participants we selected recently discussed how she knew she wanted to be a nursing home administrator ever since high school, yet "prior to the program, I never knew how to put my drive for leadership into practice." She went on to say the program helped open her eyes to the world of self-development and how "to have the yearn to do more and learn more."

Another participant admitted her greatest roadblock was her own struggles with confidence. "I knew I could be a leader," she said, "but no one ever recognized it, and I was always timid to speak up. The leadership team believing in me has allowed me to believe in me."

When you invest in your team, a natural effect is that they will want to invest in themselves. When you believe in your people, they will believe in themselves.

Now, I know all this sounds pretty, but let's do a quick cost analysis and look at the bottom line for a moment. In our industry, employee recognition programs tend to cost about $2K per person, to go toward things like seminar participation and conference presentation opportunities. Now when you compare that to the turnover cost of replacing one nurse—around $66K—it's a no-brainer. By investing in these individuals through giving them the opportunity to grow with us and *keep* them with us, we're saving $64K per individual.

Investing in yourself and investing in your team goes beyond monetary measures. At the very minimum, it's the difference between having an engaged workforce passionate about the mission and a team that barely scrapes the line of mediocrity. So treat your talent like money—don't waste it. Look for ways to invest it and—pun intended—capitalize on your human capital.

YOUR BIGGEST ASSET

On an organizational level, the concept of **Personal Human Capital** is one of the easiest to relate to GDP since it is based on the acquisition and inventory of education, skills, or talents. These are the things that you can see on a resume's "requirements" and "accomplishments" sections, such as degrees, certifications, licenses, or the accumulation of talent through years of experience.

But simply acquiring these raw assets is not enough. All the degrees in the world don't necessarily make someone the right fit. For an economy to grow, there must also be a culture present in which there are tools that allow the human capital assets to grow and thrive within the organization itself. Assessing these tools can be tricky, which is why you have to start with reflecting on your own strengths and weaknesses.

So, within the scope of P-GDP, another way to think of Human Capital is as a combination of your Natural Resources and Infrastructure for utilizing those resources. Remember, there's no elevator to success, so getting ahead of yourself or thinking you deserve a leadership role based solely on your education— or ego—will lead to failure.

There's no elevator to success, so getting ahead of yourself or thinking you deserve a leadership role based solely on your education—or ego— will lead to failure.

The foundation of Personal Human Capital is not only the education and trade skills you possess—your "book smarts"—but more importantly, your character, personality, and ability to incorporate those skills and knowledge into action—your "street smarts." The first thing a good leader should do is take stock of their own skills and knowledge and be realistic about their interests.

So now we are starting to get into the theory of making your purpose your passion. I'm a huge advocate for going after your dreams, but the reality you face before pursuing the dream is answering the questions, "Are you prepared for the journey?" And "What makes you get up in the morning?"

Not to knock the resume you've spent hours cultivating and formatting with the right font, but that's not what prepares you for the journey. And hopefully it's not the cup (or four) of coffee that makes you get up in the morning. I tell staff and my leadership all the time, "If the first reason you want to work at our organization is because it pays well or it's a paycheck, go elsewhere, because this takes a special person—a calling."

Finding your *why* won't solve all your problems or drop the perfect job into your lap, sure, but it can at least point you in the right direction. So even if you start with your *why*, you still need to honestly determine if you have the necessary skills, knowledge, and experience to turn that dream into your passion. Even if you love what you do, not every day will be filled with puppies and sunshine, but having the right skills and knowledge will equip you to get through even the hardest days and serve as a reminder it's all worth it because you'll be satisfied that you are doing what you love—and that you're making a difference.

FIVE-TOOL LEADER

In my case, I knew I wanted to be a CEO in the healthcare industry, but I knew that my path there wouldn't be as a doctor or nurse, although I have the utmost respect for those professions. Frankly, I just didn't have the natural resources to do what they do.

When looking at a baseball prospect, recruiters will sometimes refer to a gifted athlete as a "five-tool athlete," referring to the player's speed, arm strength, fielding ability, hitting for average, and hitting for power.

Over the course of baseball history, there haven't been many players that can be classified as true five-tool athletes. In fact, the most recent example would be Ken Griffey Jr., but any player who wants to be successful will look to grow in these five areas.

While there are many characteristics that we are told that good leaders need to be successful, I propose we can take the same five-tool approach to assessing Human Capital within P-GDP to measure yourself, your team, and your organization. So what does a **Five-Tool Leader** look like?

TOOL ONE: INITIATIVE

Being Italian, I have no problem taking the initiative, especially since it's aligned with the Spirit of the Immigrant that I've seen modeled all my life.

I believe you need to know when to ask for forgiveness rather than ask for permission. That being said, I see this as an earned privilege by those who have the skills and experience to make calculated risks, understanding the difference between decisive and foolhardy. I want my team to know that I trust them and feel confident enough in their skills, knowledge, and abilities to know that they can problem solve on their own so that problems can get solved faster.

One of the many reasons we started our employee recognition program was to keep our eyes on the people looking to do more than the bare minimum. Even if they aren't chosen as a participant, the application process gives us a list of those with the initiative to better themselves and—by extension—better the organization.

TOOL TWO: INNOVATIVE/CURIOSITY

There is one phrase I won't allow in my meetings: "Because that's how we've always done it." I want my team to think outside of the box or even eliminate the box entirely because I believe innovation happens when two unlike industries or minds intersect. I have always been very curious and tried to look at situations from a different angle and think differently, so I want to encourage it in others.

I mentioned in the last chapter how I had to eliminate a critical role during the course of the pandemic. At the heart of that decision, as with many difficult decisions, was the fact that sometimes individuals have a difficult time rising to the occasion and stepping up with innovative strategies and innovation.

That decision prompted us to take an innovative and curious approach to how this individual's department could move forward without anyone at its head, and now it's been reorganized. They are carrying on the innovative streak with brand new internal processes to improve the department's effectiveness.

TOOL THREE: COMPOSURE/POISE

It's easy to get emotional when you are working to achieve something that you're passionate about. I'm guilty of being emotional myself, but a good poker face can take you far, and I'm often reminded of a proverb passed down to me from both my grandfather and father: "Eyes and ears open, mouth shut," which I translate as, "Better to remain quiet and appear clueless than to speak and remove all doubt."

If you're going to lose your cool, it's got to be for the right reason, not just your own ego. In my case, it will always be in defense of my team. You can attack me all you want to, and I'll keep calm; but go after my people or my family, and it's a *whole* other story. Leaders should never hesitate to take one for the team and defend their team.

Being composed and poised means staying alert—paying attention to the verbal and nonverbal cues of others. But it also means being approachable and creating an atmosphere where people aren't afraid to bring concerns and ideas to you.

TOOL FOUR: FOCUS

The ability to keep the bigger picture in mind and see how everything fits together is critical. It doesn't matter if you're doing the day-to-day tasks, staring into the face of a deadline, or facing adversity—focus is key. I'm always telling my team, "Stay calm, stay focused, and stay positive." In fact, I really should put that on a t-shirt or coffee mug …

When a batter steps up to the plate, he's surrounded by the noise of fans either cheering or jeering at him, but his job at that moment is to focus on the pitch coming his way at ninety miles per hour. Distractions will always be around, so focus is a discipline that every leader needs to develop and display for their team.

TOOL FIVE: EMPATHETIC TEAM PLAYER

The saying is true: you are only as strong as your weakest link. This is even more true if you are a "lone leader"; you will not get far. Leadership is lonely enough as it is, so it's important to surround yourself with people smarter than you and feed off each other's abilities and talents. The one thing I have come to realize very quickly is that self-serving team members or leaders will quickly become a club of one.

An empathetic team player is able to read the situation of everyone out on the field. Going back to baseball, whenever the coach went to the mound to talk to the pitcher, he never asked, "Hey, how are you doing?" because the pitcher would never say, "I'm done—take me outta the game." If the coach wanted to know how the pitcher was doing, he'd come to me—the catcher—and ask. Why? Because I could tell from every smack of the ball against my glove how much the pitcher had left in his tank. If I said, "Yeah, coach, he's done," he knew it was an honest answer that would benefit the whole team.

I look at the Five Tools as a way to avoid both mediocrity and as a way to read the team and see the bigger picture of the kind of environment needed for Human Capital to thrive. I don't want my employees to just *manage* through a situation because "managing" means getting mired in the details and not being able to see beyond the moment. I want them to lead through it because "leading" means being able to look above the situation and take action for the best results.

I've found I can usually spot the Five Tools—or their absence—in a job candidate during the interview process simply by talking to them. That doesn't mean I always make perfect choices—there are always going to be really good BS-ers in the interview process. You're going to strike out sometimes, but a Five-Tool Leader learns from those mistakes, leaves them behind, and prepares for the next at bat, eyes focused on whatever pitch comes next.

FROM ME TO WE

When I interviewed to be CEO, I was the only candidate without senior care experience. And while I was partially chosen to bring in a fresh perspective to an organization that had posted operating losses for six straight years, that didn't excuse me from learning about the industry I was stepping into. Not by a long shot.

While I was interviewing, I started by learning about the role, getting background on the strengths and weaknesses of the organization, and seeing if the current state of my Human Capital could help fill in my gaps in experience. Beyond that, I knew I had to be honest about my lack of experience and use that to explain how I wanted to take the organization in a new direction toward sustainability while upholding a rich history and mission. Look, this was not only a board of directors I had to answer to—it was with the Sisters, and no way I was going to lie to them!

So I reviewed financials, read annual reports, and educated myself on the industry and what experts were projecting the future to look like. I did investigative work to understand who the competition was and what their organizations looked like, both financially and operationally.

As a leader, when you increase your own Human Capital, it tends to naturally bridge into making an impact on the organization. Because I had taken the time to understand the organization, after I got the job, I was able to quickly identify several areas that needed strengthening:

- Although I'm very comfortable with finance, I knew the Human Capital of the company required someone with the clear vision and focus to turn the financial misfortunes around.

- Because we are a nonprofit, I knew we required a strong development department as our foundation.

- Because I believe that our biggest capital asset was our staff, I needed strong human resources.

- But the largest piece that needed to be addressed was the clinical team, that is, our nursing staff providing the frontline care to our clients.

So I got to work immediately assessing my team's Human Capital and quickly making changes where necessary. I started with hiring someone specifically to oversee innovation and clinical operations—something that was a first not only for our organization but for the industry in our area. More changes and adjustments were made over time to include more key positions within the organization that were much needed.

Now, there is always a cost to change, but there is also a cost to *not* changing. All of these changes I was making came within the first nine months, and, after my first year, I also had a negative net operating margin. I didn't panic over it—this

> **There is always a cost to change, but there is also a cost to not changing.**

was expected. But just like in baseball, you don't just play for the inning—you play for the whole game and, more importantly, for the whole season. Sometimes you need the sacrifice fly to move a runner to score. After that first year, as our Human Capital grew, we experienced three consecutive years of net operating profits.

Personally, I realized early that I needed to work on my Personal Human Capital by measuring myself as a Five-Tool Leader. I've always been strong in the categories of **Initiative** and **Curiosity**, but as I progressed in my career, I knew I had to work harder on **Composure**, **Focus**, and **Teamwork**. I've been fortunate to observe some great leaders over the years and watch their interactions. While not all of them were Five-Tool Leaders themselves, I was able to learn something from their strengths, especially in the areas where I struggled.

For yourself, look at a past situation that you encountered and measure if you exercised the Five Tools while working through it. What did you do well? What could you have done better or differently? Would the outcome have been different if you were more composed or focused?

Professionally, assessing a team's—or team member's—Human Capital can be tricky. It takes time and practice, but if you are patient and observant, you can become skilled at evaluating it based on the Five Tools. For instance, really listening (with eyes and ears) to a person during the interview process can be very informative. The traditional interview questions are always expected by the interviewee and many times are appropriate (e.g., "What are your strengths and weaknesses?") but incorporating the concept of the Five Tools (e.g., "How did you respond the last time you were faced with a stressful situation?") will shine a different light and provide new perspective.

I'm the first to admit that I need to always be working toward becoming a Five-Tool Leader and improving my own Human Capital. So what do I do to assess my Personal Human Capital? Daily, or at least weekly, I spend time assessing myself by how I addressed situations and asking if I could have approached them in a better way. I like to use the time on my drive home to decompress, reflect on my day with a clear mind, meditate, and pray.

Remember, this hasn't always been my ritual as I had been conditioned in my previous role to go a hundred miles an hour. But sometimes we need an "Aha!" or "Ah crap!" moment to make us change, be aware, and look for those signs to change.

SELF-ASSESSMENT

So in review, the foundation of Human Capital is based on the acquisition and inventory of one's education, skills, or talents—aka your resume items. But the components that enable Human Capital to *grow* and make a wider impact are the Five Tools. It is truly the combination of these that helps you succeed, not the skills alone.

In this section, I want you to reflect on your Personal Human Capital and understand your strengths and weaknesses in light of the Five Tools.

1. I HAVE CONFIDENCE IN MY SKILLS, ABILITIES, AND KNOWLEDGE TO TAKE INITIATIVE AND ENCOURAGE OTHERS TO TAKE INITIATIVE.	
2	When facing a challenge, I feel confident in making decisive choices, and I empower others to do the same.
1	I feel confident in taking the initiative most of the time, but I don't always encourage initiative in others.
0	I can take the initiative in some areas, but I still prefer to run ideas by my supervisor first.
-1	Taking the initiative makes me feel anxious as I'm worried about doing the wrong thing.
-2	I'm not sure I've ever taken the initiative in my work, nor have I been encouraged to do so.

It's important to know the difference between initiative and self-interest. Initiative is a form of confidence in your own Human Capital, not just doing whatever you want because you can. More importantly, your ability to take the initiative should translate to others feeling confident in their ability to take decisive action.

2. I APPROACH ALL ASPECTS OF MY WORK WITH A SENSE OF CURIOSITY AND A DESIRE TO INNOVATE.

2	I enjoy looking at things from new angles, trying out new ideas, and challenging the status quo.
1	I have the desire to innovate, but mostly in areas that are obvious problems.
0	I'm willing to try some changes and new ideas in increments, but I struggle to see curiosity as a positive thing.
-1	I'm anxious about how changes will disrupt things and create more work for me and my team.
-2	I tend to value consistency over change, even if I know change could improve things.

Curiosity didn't kill the cat … stupidity did. Curiosity can actually be seen as cautious creativity—looking at an old problem in a new way, experimenting to find the greatest results. Sometimes turning upside-down gives you a whole new perspective—or it might show you that you are already doing things the best way.

3. I AM ABLE TO MAINTAIN COMPOSURE AND POISE IN THE FACE OF CHALLENGES AND OPPOSITION.

2	When met with resistance, I am always able to keep my responses in check and others find me approachable.
1	I am poised and composed most of the time unless it's a personal attack.
0	I know how to keep my cool so long as the other person is able to do the same.
-1	I typically reflect back the same emotions I see in others.
-2	I tend to wear my feelings on my sleeve and others appear hesitant to approach me because of my reactions and responses.

Maybe you've heard the expression "be a thermostat, not a thermometer." It's not just good personal advice, but it also translates well within Human Capital. The composed leader is able to keep their focus on the bigger picture and remain receptive to input from others instead of interpreting pushback as a personal attack.

4. I AM FOCUSED ON HOW I NEED TO GROW MY HUMAN CAPITAL IN LIGHT OF THE BIGGER PICTURE.	
2	I am actively growing my abilities, skills, and knowledge, and I encourage others by providing opportunity and resources for them to grow too.
1	I know the areas in which I need to grow my Human Capital but still need to gain more clarity and focus on how to do so.
0	I have some idea of where I need to expand my Human Capital but lack the opportunities to focus on doing so.
-1	Growing my Human Capital is not a priority right now because there are too many other things taking my attention.
-2	I have no idea where to start with growing my Human Capital and cannot easily focus on my why.

Remember, focus is about more than just paying attention. It's understanding *why* you do what you do so that you have the clarity to grow your Human Capital and encourage growth in others.

	5. I UTILIZE EMPATHY TO ENCOURAGE TEAMWORK AND SUPPORT MY TEAM FOR THE GREATEST RESULTS.
2	I believe that a team is only as strong as its weakest link, therefore I keep a close watch on the pulse of the team and actively look for ways to serve and support them.
1	I have a strong personal sense of teamwork, but I need to do more to encourage the same spirit in our organization as a whole.
0	I know teamwork is important, but I do not currently have tools in place to proactively encourage and build it.
-1	Teamwork is a good topic to revisit and emphasize once or twice a year, but I don't think about it in day-to-day life.
-2	My organization has more internal competition than collaboration, and I am not sure how to correct that.

No one is perfect—and that's why we need each other. No matter how many books I read, podcasts I listen to, or conferences I attend, there will always be gaps in my knowledge and abilities, so I look to surround myself with people with different strengths. Building a strong team actually bolsters my Human Capital and gives me the chance to enhance their Human Capital.

CONCLUSION

Kris Bryant, third baseman for the Chicago Cubs (as of the writing of this book), is the only player in the history of baseball to win college player of the year, minor league player of the year, Rookie of the Year, and Most Valuable Player over four consecutive years, 2013 to 2016. Oh—and 2016 was also the year the Cubs won the World Series for the first time since 1908.

In terms of "Baseball Capital," you won't find many others with a better resume. But in a recent interview, Bryant discussed his struggles with losing his love for the game of baseball. The criticism from fans, trade rumors, injuries, and contract disputes seem to have chipped away at his passion.

Here's a guy living out his lifelong dream of playing professional sports with the greatest resources available to him, and yet he's lost the joy in it. If nothing else, this proves that Human Capital goes beyond the raw skills and knowledge and must also include your passion. The closer you are to your *why*, the more passionate you are to grow your Human Capital.

I mention this because no matter whether you are a new manager or a CEO, there is an expiration date on your job. There will come a day when you wake up and realize that you just don't love what you do anymore. It's not about having a bad day or week but realizing that you've lost the "love of the game." At that point, the honest and best thing to do is to move on—to another role or another organization.

I've seen too many people stay put in jobs and organizations past their expiration date because they don't want to walk away from the big paycheck. But they weren't making any kind of impact anymore as they had lost interest in the *human* part of Human Capital. At the end of the day, the closer you are to your *why*, the more passionate you are to grow your Human Capital, and the closer you are to being a kick-asset leader.

CHAPTER 5

TECHNOLOGY

The great myth of our times is that technology is communication.
— *LIBBY LARSEN*

When I was going through twelve grueling rounds of chemotherapy, I can still remember being in tears while the nurse would stand there, arm around me, hugging me, stroking my hair. And of course, my parents were there for me too, both during the treatment and then at home while I would lie awake at night in agony or throwing up my guts in the bathroom. I can tell you firsthand that there's a reason no one ever describes chemo as glamorous.

Technology helped me survive, no doubt about it—but so did the human touch I felt through the compassion and care I received. To this day, I believe that problems are not solved by advancements in technology but through the empathy and conviction of human beings. That's why people are—and always will be—your greatest asset.

We have had the honor and privilege of caring for some truly remarkable people, seniors who have made significant contributions in both their lives and the community—even the nation and world. From athletes to politicians to media personalities and, most of all, our veterans, the one thing I am extremely proud of is the fact that we treat all residents with the same compassion and level of care regardless of who they are.

When I first became CEO, I was on the welcome trail, getting to know people and introducing myself. One man I wanted to meet was Frank Fuhrer Jr., who had built and operated a successful business in Western Pennsylvania for years. I knew of Frank from not only his successful beverage distribution company but also for his generosity throughout our community in various philanthropic endeavors. Success had not come easily for him—he tried and failed and faced adversity, but he chose his hard and followed the values he believed and found his great and turned it into success and happiness, paying it forward through his generosity. So—somewhat selfishly—I wanted to learn more from a man who has been around the block a few times and who I knew would have words of wisdom for me as a new CEO.

I recall a mutual friend calling me once they found out I was meeting with him to make sure that I was clean-shaven, wore a suit and tie, and shined my shoes. I understand that times have changed and today the work environment has become more casual, but Frank was a leader who wanted certain things a certain way, and I respected that.

As I arrived at Frank B. Fuhrer Wholesale Co. headquarters on the South Side of Pittsburgh, my first reaction was "Damn, this is a large operation." In fact, the operations covered over twenty-four acres and five buildings that totaled over 370,000 square feet. I drove up to the entrance, and a friendly guard introduced himself and instructed me to park in one of the visitor spaces. I thought, "What a great first impression!"

As I walked to the office building, I caught sight of a large monument with Frank's picture and an inscription that read:

INTEGRITY—FAIRNESS—CONSISTENCY

These Philosophies are the Cornerstone on Which Our Company Was Founded and Has Prospered

"The Meaning of my Life is to help others find the meaning of theirs."
FRANK B. FUHRER

I had read about Frank and his style, and while some thought it was a little harsh, I admired his style because it was very up-front and you knew where you stood.

I was met by Frank's assistant and taken to his office where I was greeted by Frank with a firm handshake, a warm smile, and direct eye contact. As we sat down at a small table, Frank came straight out and asked, "So how much money are you here to ask for?"

I was confused because that was not my intention at all, and I answered him with, "Frank, I'm not here to ask you for anything but your time and wisdom, and to congratulate you on your success."

Now *he* was confused! Most people come to ask for something of monetary value, but I wanted something more valuable: his wisdom he had gained through failure and success in his life.

We sat and talked for about an hour, and it was as if I was talking to an old friend, like I was having a conversation with my grandfather. Frank was very gracious with his time, and for that hour, there was no email, no texts, no interruptions. It was something I will never forget because I noticed his stories all came back to that monument: "Integrity, Fairness, and Consistency."

But most importantly, Frank repeated to me the quote from that monument: "The meaning of my life is to help others find the meaning of theirs."

Toward the end of our meeting, he reached into a box and gave me one of the first copies of his book, *Let's Be Frank*, signed it, and thanked me for my work.

Right about now you might be wondering, "Nick, that's great—but what in the world does this have to do with technology?" After all, the simple human action of a handshake—the combination of human touch while looking straight into someone's eyes to forge a connection—doesn't involve any technology as we generally think about it.

In any line of work, technology is essential to getting the job done and remaining competitive. That's just a fact, and it's especially true in healthcare where technology can literally be the difference between life and death. But I like to think of technology in two categories: High Tech and Low Tech. High Tech represents the traditional electronics-based view of technology, Low Tech represents the human touch.

> I like to think of technology in two categories: High Tech and Low Tech. High Tech represents the traditional electronics-based view of technology, Low Tech represents the human touch.

There will always be new High-Tech tools to invest in—the latest computers and software—but there is simply no replacement for Low Tech.

That day started with uncertainty, the uncertainty of living up to the standard that Frank Fuhrer had for people he met. It ended with a handshake, hug, and the start of a friendship with one of the most influential men in my city. Through failures and success, Frank was able to find his great, and when he did, he was willing to share that story with many through his book—but more importantly, he shared it in person with a young, impressionable CEO. And for that, I will forever be grateful.

PERSONAL TECHNOLOGY

Where Human Capital within Personal GDP is very similar to Human Capital in GDP, we have to approach Technology from a slightly different angle with P-GDP. With GDP, technology is primarily measured in the growth and development of a country based upon its technological resources and capabilities. But with P-GDP, technology has to be measured in the human impact (Low Tech) that can be made through High Tech.

At the end of the day, both have this in common: the human aspect (Low Tech) is what drives the High Tech. In today's world, it can be easy for leaders to justify hiding behind technology and become overdependent upon it for communication. Instead, we need leaders that can embrace their humanity by being approachable, empathetic, authentic, trustworthy, and honest. You can't get that from technology alone.

Although the measure of technology within the economic parameters of GDP may be focused more on the end product, within P-GDP, the definition of technology must be focused on the human aspects of touch, communications, and interaction. So yes, I know you can use your phone and email for communicating, that you can create complex data sets, or that you have thousands of online followers, but put that crap away and talk to me from the *heart*. Can you do *that* well? How Low Tech are you?

This question becomes especially relevant if you are in the millennial and Generation Z groups coming into leadership. In a 2018 study,

55 percent of millennial bosses reported that electronic messaging (i.e., Microsoft Teams) was their preferred way to communicate with their direct reports.[6] Meanwhile, Gen X bosses relied heavily on email, and Baby Boomers still preferred face-to-face.[7] While High-Tech tools can increase the immediacy of communication, the importance and significance of human touch and interaction is and always will be powerful. Tech cannot convey pure emotion, genuineness, or feeling that gets lost in a text or DM.

THE HIGH-TECH/LOW-TECH CONNECTION

High Tech has provided extraordinary advancements in medicine and manufacturing but also communications. Communication has evolved over thousands of years from cave drawing, hieroglyphics, writing letters, telephones, and today, the ability to video conference and chat virtually. When we think of communication today, it's impossible not to think of social media and other electronics-based technologies that enable the sharing of ideas, thoughts, and information. After all, we now live in the age of AE … Artificial Emotions.

Communication has always required tools—whether a chisel against stone—or a keyboard and Wi-Fi connection—but communication itself requires human behavior to accomplish. In that way, technology today is no different—the human touch is central to

---

6   "Millennials as Bosses: Forget Face-to-Face, Online Messaging New Norm for Communicating with Direct Reports, According to Korn Ferry Survey" Business Wire, March 12, 2018, https://www.businesswire.com/news/home/20180312005112/en/Millennials-as-Bosses-Forget-Face-to-Face-Online-Messaging-New-Norm-for-Communicating-with-Direct-Reports-According-to-Korn-Ferry-Survey.

7   "The Evolution of Communication Across Generations," Notre Dame of Maryland University, February 6, 2019, https://online.ndm.edu/news/communication/evolution-of-communication/.

communication happening, no matter the medium. In today's world of virtual meetings and video conferencing, technology is vital, but humans still have the control of *how* that meeting goes, the overall vibe and interaction.

In fact, one might argue that now is definitely not the time to skimp on the High-Tech capabilities that allow Low Tech to thrive. In this view, High Tech cannot be seen as an end in and of itself but rather as a way to enable and empower Low Tech and Human Capital.

LOW-TECH INVESTMENT

According to a 2016 analysis of high-tech spending, it was found that countries worldwide were spending "close to $6 trillion a year" on combined technology needs. Viewing that number in terms of GDP would make the "technology economy" the third largest in the world, sitting between the economies of China and Japan.[8]

Likewise, organizations have to invest in their technology to remain competitive, to serve clients, and to be productive. When it comes to your organization, you really don't need me to lecture you on the importance of investing in your high tech, but how much investment is going into the Low-Tech aspect? And what does it look like to invest in your Low Tech?

As a leader, I've learned that no amount of high tech can replace the feeling you get from a word or encouragement or face-to-face recognition for a job well done. It's difficult to convey authenticity, sincerity, tone, and passion through high-tech channels, but when you're looking someone in the eye and shaking a hand, the full weight of it can be felt. Plus, I think most of us have been on the receiving

---

8   Marco Antonio Cavallo, "The Growing Importance of the Technology Economy," *CIO*, December 21, 2016, https://www.cio.com/article/3152568/the-growing-importance-of-the-technology-economy.html.

end of backlash resulting from a misunderstood text or email that could have been easily avoided in a personal conversation.

One of the ways that I've decided to invest in my own Low Tech was through hosting a series of Breakfast with the CEO events. It was really important to me to better understand the concerns among our staff, especially those on the frontline—face to face, person to person.

Now, when I first brought up this idea to my leadership, they suggested a High-Tech solution: send out a survey to the staff, collect the anonymous responses, filter those responses, and then the results would be brought back for me to review.

But that was exactly the opposite of what I wanted. I didn't want a High-Tech solution for a Low-Tech problem. Instead, I decided I didn't want the rest of my leadership involved at all. I didn't want feedback filtered through what they thought was important for me to hear … or filtered by what they *wanted* me to hear.

So I decided to take what I called the "Vegas Approach," meaning that I led off each breakfast by telling the staff that what was said in the room would stay in the room, granting them immunity from any kind of disciplinary actions that could've come up from my leadership being involved. They could dump the whole ugly truth on me.

And by taking this approach … I *got* the whole ugly truth. I heard complaints of low pay that my leadership would've probably filtered out because "Everyone complains they are paid too little." Instead, I got to hear the story behind the complaints—stories of staff working multiple jobs to care for their family. Some might ask, "Then why not leave for a job that can pay you better?" And the simple answer that came back over and over was "Because I love our residents. Because I believe we're making a difference."

They could walk away from the pay … they couldn't walk away from the *people*. And these were exactly the kind of people I needed to keep on our team—people who put mission before money. You can train anyone to use High Tech ... but I needed the kind of people with the Low Tech to care for our residents.

From these meetings, I was able to pick up on culture issues and problems that a survey would've never been able to identify and start working toward solutions, such as our current plan to pay a living wage so staff can pursue better work-life balance by spending time with their families instead of spending that time at a second (or even third) job just to keep food on the table.

I'm not going to lie—this was a draining and time-consuming exercise. But it was worth it. Now it's become a standard practice for our leadership team, and we've tweaked it so that I won't be doing it alone, but every member of my leadership will "do the rounds" and have breakfast with different teams and hear from them face to face. I think it's worth noting too that I didn't come up with this idea on my own overnight; these were practices I learned through the many roles I'd had in my healthcare career through various organizations I'd worked for.

We've also developed around twenty working groups within the company to tackle issues that might otherwise go under the radar. For example, we have a working group devoted to renovations, and we can't have just administrators in there talking about what they think needs fixing—we need nurses and housekeepers in there because they see *everything*. These groups meet weekly to get input from each other in ways that would never come up—or get lost—in an email chain.

Beyond myself and our staff, we're continuing to find other ways to invest in our Low-Tech capabilities. We had identified a lack of interest among medical field students in working in geriatrics. To address this problem, we've partnered with a local university to start an intergenerational program at one of our personal care homes.

Each semester, we accept fifteen graduate students in the field of health sciences and offer them a reduced level of rent. As part of their studies, there are High-Tech aspects like conducting clinical assessments with our seniors but also a Low-Tech side, like conversing with the seniors and doing activities together. These programs are not proprietary or even new—they are occurring at many places around the world—but they were new to us.

From an investment perspective, I believe every organization should be putting seventy cents of every dollar of their budget into Human Capital. While much of that will include salaries, within that should be specific line items for how Low Tech will be enhanced— things like Breakfast with the CEO, employee recognition, learning opportunities, staff picnics—anything that is designed to intentionally encourage human interaction.

Like anything else we've discussed in Personal GDP, this has to start with *you*. Actions speak a lot louder than words. So your website can claim your staff is your most important asset or that customer care is your greatest priority, but that's all just BS if your budget and strategy don't show clear actions being taken in those areas.

SELF-ASSESSMENT

In many ways, this section is going to piggyback on your assessment regarding Human Capital because there is such an overlap between your skills and abilities and how those empower your ability to communicate and connect with others through Low Tech.

Ultimately, you have to lead by example through placing an importance on social skills that then trickles down through the organization in how other managers interact with their teams and the financial investment reflected in your Human Capital.

1. MY PREFERRED AND PREDOMINANT MEANS OF COMMUNICATION ARE THROUGH TEXT, EMAIL, MESSAGING, RATHER THAN FACE TO FACE.

2	Not at all—I use technological means to support the communication that happens through human touch. I use High Tech to help me have more human interaction (i.e., video conference), and I actively encourage others to do the same.
1	I certainly prefer face-to-face contact, but I have not taken intentional steps to foster a culture where this is being emulated in my organization.
0	I use High Tech means of communicating with most people in the organization and reserve Low Tech means for my C-Suite or board of directors, etc.
-1	High Tech is my preferred means of communication, but I'll make exceptions when it is best for me. I'm doubtful how I could be more productive through more Low-Tech interactions.
-2	I prefer using High Tech in every situation, and if I could avoid all face-to-face meetings, I would do so. I'm just too busy for that kind of interaction.

Now, for our purposes, I'm counting video conferencing as a form of face-to-face communication. To me, this is the best use of High Tech—when it enables and empowers Low-Tech connections. Even if you are unable to meet in person, it still helps you pick up on personal cues—tone, nonverbal communication—that could never be achieved through an email.

Ultimately, you have to lead by example through placing an importance on social skills that then trickles down through the organization in how other managers interact with their teams.

2. I SPEND MORE TIME ENGAGED ON SOCIAL MEDIA THAN IN ACTUAL CONVERSATION OR HUMAN INTERACTION.

2	No—I make sure that the majority of my interactions are through human contact so that I can look someone in the eye, hear their tone, and build a real relationship with them.
1	I believe I spend more time in human interaction, but I admit that social media is a common distraction that pulls me away from human touch.
0	I probably spend an equal amount of time between social media and human interaction, but I should look for ways to shift the balance to human engagement.
-1	I definitely spend more time on social media than I do engaging in human conversation, and I haven't given much thought to why or how this should change.
-2	Honestly, I prefer to keep my interactions on social media because I find it less draining and less time-consuming than human interaction.

Social media is addictive. I'm guilty of FOMO when it comes to social media—fear that I'm going to miss some essential business news, a sports trade, or notification from a friend. But this was making me miss out on the low-tech side of life. My daughter has called me out for paying more attention to my phone when I should have been paying attention to *her*. It probably won't be much longer before I'm begging her to put down her phone and pay attention to *me*!

	3. I FIND TWO HOURS EVERY DAY TO "UNPLUG" FROM HIGH TECH SO THAT I CAN FOCUS ON LOW-TECH INTERACTIONS.
2	I make sure to have at least two hours every day to set aside High Tech and invest in human contact, both personally and professionally, and I encourage others to do the same.
1	While I do set aside time to unplug, it's probably not two hours. I'm conscious of the benefit of separating myself from High Tech and spending time in Low-Tech interactions.
0	I know I need to unplug more, but I don't know where to start on making that happen and have not put anything into practice yet.
-1	I'm afraid I'll miss something important if I set aside technology. I put more importance on the information I get electronically than on what I get via human connection.
-2	I'm never unplugged and don't have any plans to change that.

I know this question can be challenging because I also struggle with when I should be "plugged in" to make sure I'm available for my team. It's not practical to set aside an hour of the day as "email/phone call time" because that's just not how life works, and I believe a quick response time can be a way to show care for my team—again, a High-Tech way to be Low Tech.

So I think it has to start with you developing an "unplugged culture" by establishing clear expectations for your team: "This is my unplugged time, so please know that you will not get a quick response during this time frame." Have a backup plan: who is going to field emergency calls for you during your unplugged time? If you don't make the plan, no one is going to make it for you.

	4. MY DOLLAR INVESTMENT IN HIGH TECH IS LESS THAN MY INVESTMENT IN HUMAN CAPITAL.
2	On a personal level, I spend more of my money on growing my Human Capital rather than the latest gadget. On a professional level, I make sure 70 percent of our budget is directed toward employees through salary and benefits.
1	I spend my dollars more on Low Tech and Human Capital in one area of my life (Personal or Professional) but not the other half.
0	I would say my investment is closer to fifty-fifty, but I recognize that I need to invest more in Human Capital and Low Tech.
-1	Having the latest and greatest tech is important to me, both personally and professionally and is a bigger focus to me than Human Capital needs.
-2	I struggle to see the benefit of investing more resources in Human Capital/Low Tech because I place a higher value on High-Tech needs and wants.

If you really want to make sure you are honest with answering this question, ask yourself this: is it easier for you to justify spending $1500 on the latest smartphone than it is for you to justify spending $10 a month for a gym membership or $200 to attend a leadership conference? Feeling a little bit guilty yet? Good.

Too many leaders focus on being "cutting edge" by investing more in High Tech than in people, which leads to their people living "on the edge." Don't get me wrong—it can feel great to have the latest tech and show it off. But money doesn't lie, and it will show where you place a greater emphasis, both for yourself and for your organization.

	5. I AM USING HIGH TECH TO FOSTER LOW-TECH CONNECTIVITY AND GROWTH.
2	High Tech is not an end in and of itself but a way to benefit Low-Tech aspects of life, especially empowering the human touch.
1	I mostly use High Tech to benefit Low Tech, but I am not actively encouraging others to do the same.
0	I don't always think about the connection between High Tech and Low Tech, but I recognize I need to analyze this more in myself and my organization.
-1	I focus more energy and time on utilizing High Tech for myself, but I struggle to see how I can use it to benefit Low-Tech areas of my life and work.
-2	I use High Tech to avoid Low-Tech interactions rather than look for ways it can benefit human touch.

Since the dawn of mankind, we've used tools to make our lives better, and High Tech is no different. But we have to be watchful of crossing a line where High Tech ends up making our lives more complicated, more disconnected, and less productive. Look, these questions are challenging for me too—and a good reminder that I have to be intentional in being Low Tech.

CONCLUSION

Technology naturally overlaps with every element of Personal GDP we've discussed so far. I know I've already asked a bunch of questions, but I think we always need to be asking ourselves the same questions over and over when it comes to Technology within P-GDP:

- How is technology helping me use my natural resources?

- How is technology helping me identify and fulfill my needs in Health and Infrastructure?

- How is technology helping me develop my Human Capital?

- How is technology helping me be more productive?

I'm not here to warn you that High Tech is evil or that it's going to destroy us like some kind of *Terminator* meets *The Matrix* doomsday scenario—though, let's be honest, I'd probably pay to see that movie. But I do think that on the stairway to success, we have to assess whether we are focusing enough on our Low-Tech capabilities and how High Tech can bring about the greatest good. As important as technology is for productivity, being tech-savvy will only get you so far if you can't be human-savvy.

CHAPTER 6
PRODUCTIVITY

Never mistake motion for action.
— *ERNEST HEMINGWAY*

Early in my career when I was a financial analyst for a major hospital, I learned one of the most valuable lessons of my career. At five o'clock every day, my boss would come by my cubicle, and if I didn't turn off the computer myself, he'd reach over and turn it off for me.

First time this happened, I couldn't believe it. *What's happening? How rude! Crap ... did I save that file?*

His reasoning was simple: "Look, we're not surgeons or physicians here. We don't have a chest cracked wide open in front of us that needs to be fixed right now. So if you're staying here until six o'clock with the amount of work that I know I gave you, either you're trying to kiss up—and I don't like a kiss-up—or you don't know what you're doing."

This was, of course, completely contrary to my expectation that I show up early every day and stay late every day to prove that I was productive. But there's a quote I love that says, "Just because you are doing something doesn't mean it's worthwhile."

That interaction taught me a simple truth: there's a huge difference between keeping busy and being productive. And beyond that, the sense of fulfillment in a task is more important than the task itself.

Recently, I got the chance to pass this idea on to my son. We spend a couple hours of father-son time every Sunday morning car spotting, and as we drove around one morning, he shared with me that many of his social media followers lament their failures and lack of accomplishments.

"How do you define a failure?" I asked him.

His explanation was straightforward enough: "It's a failure if I don't get something done or done right."

When we got home, I had him do a small exercise: I asked him to look back on the last two days and write down everything he accomplished along with his "to do" list and compare. At the end, he was able to identify twenty-five items he'd accomplished. In fact, the only items he hadn't completed were the assignments that weren't due until the following week.

Suddenly, he perked up, and his mood changed. The past two days, he had been so focused on what was left "to do" that he hadn't been able to celebrate what had been done.

Most of us need to make this shift in mindset in how we view productivity; we focus so much on a task list and how much there is left to do that we neglect to stop and consider whether we're even doing the right things. Because when you do the right things, it will lead you into greater satisfaction in your work *and* more productivity. True productivity is the result of choosing a hard and focusing on it, which will ultimately help you produce happiness and success.

PERSONAL PRODUCTIVITY

Now, we find ourselves at the peak of the P-GDP pyramid, where Productivity represents the combination of everything that comes before it: Natural Resources, Health and Infrastructure, Human Capital, and Technology.

Within the context of GDP, productivity measures a nation's workforce, the unemployment rate, whether the labor force is employed, and what labor needs are still available. When we relate this to Personal GDP, however, we have to look not just at whether you are steadily employed but how satisfied and fulfilled you are in your work.

Personal Productivity is the natural result of a person, team, or workforce that is truly engaged, not the result of merely filling roles with warm bodies to go through the motions.

I propose that Personal Productivity is the natural result of a person, team, or workforce that is truly engaged, not the result of merely filling roles with warm bodies to go through the motions.

For starters, let's take a walk through a day in the life of a traditionally "productive" individual, whose behaviors cascade down to the team and ultimately the organization. See if this outline of the "average day" looks or sounds familiar:

AVERAGE DAY	
TIME	**TASK**
7:00 A.M.	The day starts before you even get to work by checking phone messages, texts, and emails.
8:00 A.M.	Get your first cup of coffee, sit down, start to prioritize your to do list for the day.
9:00 A.M.	Grab your second cup of coffee, get back to your desk, check various social media to make sure you aren't missing anything your connections are up to.
9:30 A.M.	All right, now you're ready to start tackling the projects at hand! But you can't get started; you need some inspiration and can't seem to get your brain to work, so you make an attempt at productivity by at least appearing busy.
10:00 A.M.	Just when you thought you were being productive and knocked out a couple of tasks, fire number one comes at you—and it needs to be done twenty minutes ago. This throws everything off. The day's now shot ...
11:00 A.M.	All this stress has made you lose focus. What were you working on before the emergency? Oh well ... time for coffee number three, a cookie, cupcake, or maybe you just go straight to the hard stuff. Chocolate, that is.
12:00 P.M.	Ah, lunch. Just in time. But wait ... you have a lunch meeting. Between bites, you jot down several new tasks that now need to be dealt with ASAP.
1:00 P.M.	On the bright side, your blood sugar's up and you have a burst of productivity and get several things crossed off the list. Now we're talking!
2:00 P.M.	Uh-oh. There's that inspirational block again ... the deer in the headlights stare on your face. Since you're stuck, you head back to social media ... maybe your connections can offer some inspiration. While you're there, you might as well check emails and texts, and a cat video can probably help.

2:30 P.M.	You've got a meeting coming up, and you've got to prep for it. Grab a snack, another cup of coffee to make sure you're on your A-game, and where did you save that presentation file?
4:30 P.M.	Your video call ran over and just as it ended, a "quick" request came your way. It shouldn't take too long to complete ... An hour and a half later, it's done.
6:00 P.M.	Wow, look at the time! You've got to get home to the family/significant other/pet. You'll just check social media and email one last time before calling it a day because you'll be in traffic and don't want to miss anything. You'll get to the priority list tomorrow. What a crazy busy day!

Feel free to sprinkle in some small talk or an additional meeting or two (or three) along with the call from home about dinner, soccer, or school. This gets repeated over and over and although this seems like a busy and "productive" day, was it really?

Moment of truth: I can raise my hand and say I've had too many days that look just like this. In some ways, it's easier to just show up and go through the motions, settling for the mediocre and mundane, rather than to introduce more stress by pursuing your passion. It's true that if you set expectations low, you will never be disappointed … except in the long run.

QUALITY NOT QUANTITY

Obviously, I'm not a fan of gauging my productivity by a task list. After all, real life is full of emergencies, and it only takes one of those to completely derail the task list. Instead, I propose leaders do a 180 and create an *accomplishments* list. Please don't misunderstand me— yes, I'm aware there are daily required activities that you need to get done, but those don't equate to accomplishments.

I keep a daily/weekly/monthly/annual accomplishments list to understand, beyond my job requirements, what else was I able to accomplish? There are many days when I feel like I have done absolutely nothing of impact until I reflect back and realize I actually did more important work than what was on my task list.

A leader's day will be filled with making decisions, giving advice, providing perspective, mentoring, setting direction, and bringing clarity—but these things can't be put on any list; they just come with the role. If you are a good leader, these activities will be plentiful as people will come to you; they will follow you because they want to, not because they have to.

So then, we have to move away from measuring success as a leader by the quantity of what gets done and instead by the quality of what gets done. Personally, my issue is that I want to do more than the generations before me. I feel like I owe it to them for all the sacrifices they made for me, and nobody remembers mediocrity.

P-GDP Productivity is about productive fulfillment, not just output. Countries are competing in a world market against other countries and jockeying to make the best product at the lowest cost, which yields the most favorable margin, but that does not always translate to happiness. If countries, organizations, and leaders understood this concept, they would realize that happiness inspires productivity. Imagine the levels of true productivity fulfillment that could be achieved!

The goal of a leader should be to make a mark on this world by leaving behind something extraordinary.

Therefore, the goal of a leader should be to make a mark on this world by leaving behind something extraordinary. You can run on a treadmill where the scenery never changes, or you can get out and discover your life. Why settle for the mediocrity of the rat race when you can contribute something to the human race?

STRATEGY TO PRODUCTIVITY

So how do you change your scenery and work toward not just productivity but toward engagement and personal fulfillment? To do that, you're going to have to be prepared to rethink your beliefs about productivity and be open to shifting your mindset, whatever it currently is. It's not going to happen by accident, but you can take strategic steps that will lead you into being more engaged and productive in your work.

As I mentioned earlier in the book, I worked for a wonderful healthcare organization where I gained a ton of experience, but I reached a point where my days emulated the vicious cycle of the "average day." I was becoming someone that I did not want to be— professionally or personally.

I did not realize that was happening until my daughter, who was seven at the time, gave me a reality check. As a school assignment, she was supposed to draw a picture of family time activities. She pointed and said, "Daddy, these are your favorite activities: you like going to work in that big building, and you always have the phone with you, and when you come home, you're on your laptop." Ouch. I have to tell you ... I never thought my life lesson would come from my seven-year-old, but it did.

STEP ONE: RECOGNIZE MEDIOCRITY AND MAKE CHANGES

Ditch the "average day" filled with mediocre tasks and make changes that start with *you*. Many times, we become paralyzed by comfort. We don't fear the change itself but the unknown that follows the change.

Change means there will be some discomfort in the beginning, but that's where you get to choose your hard. Here's the thing—you might choose the wrong type of change at some point. That's okay—at least you're moving away from mediocrity and toward finding your great.

STEP TWO: IDENTIFY WHAT YOU CARE ABOUT

There may be many changes you make, but the biggest will be to find something you truly care about. For me, I was stuck in the "another day, another dollar" mentality — or as my grandfather used to say, "another day, another fifty cents but with inflation." My work was no longer a reflection of something I could be proud of, a feeling of fulfillment. I needed to have a reason to work hard by making an impact, not just move widgets for a living. I had to wake up every morning and be reinvigorated by what I was doing and why I was doing it. I needed purpose, not just a paycheck.

When you find what you care about, that doesn't mean you'll go home every day bouncing around like a toddler who just found his mom's candy stash. When I go home after a long day, I'm often mentally and physically exhausted. I still have good days and bad, but the good heavily outweighs the bad—and I can find good that happened even in the bad days. When you truly care about the work, the tired feeling is more like finishing a great workout—you're sore, but you feel good about it because you were productive. When you are passionate about what you do, work should not feel like work, and there is a significant correlation between happiness and productivity.

STEP THREE: LOVE WHAT YOU DO

In the same way that busyness doesn't convert to fulfillment, hard work doesn't necessarily mean you love what you do. Passion for what you do (Step 2) is not the same as *loving* what you do.

For example, I have seen where a nurse is very good at his or her calling and is passionate about caring for residents. But once they are thrust into a supervisory role … they realize that they lack the passion for leadership and everything that comes along with it.

Now, maybe you've already figured these things out. If you have, then it's time to execute your plan and maintain focus. It's easy to get distracted from your strategy, but I've personally found the following best practices helpful.

BEST PRACTICE 1: SELF-DISCIPLINE

The only thing you can control is yourself. No one knows better than you what distractions are the most tempting to *you*. But it also means sticking to the rules you set yourself. To go back to the last chapter, if you set aside a daily time to unplug, then you need the self-discipline to actually unplug during that time!

It also means being consistent in how you assess what is really an emergency you need to respond to. Just because it feels like an emergency to someone else doesn't mean it actually is. A leader has to have the self-discipline to be the calm one, take a step back, and say, "Is this really a fire? Or can it wait until tomorrow?" You may just be able to turn it into a teaching moment for your staff.

BEST PRACTICE 2: PLAN AHEAD
FOR EMERGENCIES

Now, if it actually is an emergency, that's fine—deal with it. But you can't live in a continual state of crisis if you are going to be productive. You have to plan ahead for emergencies. Sure, you'll never know exactly what they will be, but you can safely assume they will come along. That being the case, create space in your schedule to deal with emergencies and have a team member you trust to step in for you. And if you have that rare emergency-free day, wonderful! You can use that time to work on strategy or team care or help out a team member.

BEST PRACTICE 3: TAKE A BREAK

Self-discipline doesn't mean just putting your head down and keeping your nose to the grindstone. Multiple studies have shown that taking regular, short breaks actually *boosts* productivity. In one such study, it was found that "the ideal work rhythm was fifty-two minutes of work time followed by a seventeen-minute break."[9]

In addition, the same study found that the most effective breaks were ones in which you completely disconnect from work: standing up, going for a walk, reading a book (for fun, not work), listening to music, talking with colleagues about life … and other things that human beings do. In addition to making you more productive, it's also good for your mental and physical health. Go figure!

---

9   Minda Zetlin, "For the Most Productive Workday, Science Says Make Sure to Do This," *Inc.*, March 21, 2019, https://www.inc.com/minda-zetlin/productivity-workday-52-minutes-work-17-minutes-break-travis-bradberry-pomodoro-technique.html.

BEST PRACTICE 4: HAVE NO EXPECTATIONS

Easier said than done, right? This is an entire mindset shift—to approach each day as a blank slate. Yes, you may have a calendar full of meetings and deadlines, but this is more about not putting undue stress and worry on yourself.

I learned from a wise Sister how worry consumes our time needlessly. She said, "I try not to worry about things because sometimes those worries never materialize."

Think about that: how much time do we waste worrying about things that never happen? According to a study conducted by Penn State, researchers found that 91 percent of worries never materialized, and for one in four of the study participants, *none* of their worries came true.[10]

BEST PRACTICE 5: RECAP YOUR DAY

Instead of starting the day with the task list and potentially setting yourself up for failure, end the day with a recap of what was done. What were your wins? What could have gone better? What did you learn? Who did you help? These are the accomplishments that are going to have a long-term impact beyond the day itself and lead to more productivity and fulfillment.

In the end, it all goes back to what my son and I talked about—tossing the list and measuring your day by the impact of what you did, not by what you didn't do. Another baseball analogy for you: a closer in baseball is not paid for the number of pitches he throws, but he's paid for making the save. Whether that takes three pitches or forty pitches, the save is what matters. In fact, the less pitches, the more efficient—and productive—the pitcher is. Again, quality over quantity!

---

10   Seth J. Gillihan, "How Often Do Your Worries Actually Come True?" *Psychology Today*, July 19, 2019, https://www.psychologytoday.com/us/blog/think-act-be/201907/how-often-do-your-worries-actually-come-true.

THREE LEVELS OF ENGAGEMENT

While different companies will define and measure employee engagement differently, there's one thing that stays the same: engagement leads to productivity. In fact, studies have shown that "companies with high employee engagement are 21% more profitable" and that engaged workplaces saw as much as "41% less absenteeism" among their workforce.[11]

In my own observations, I've identified three levels of employee engagement that a leader can use to gauge themselves and their workforce.

Think of your organization like the food pyramid, where your goal is to have a solid base of healthy foods that you eat frequently and bad or unhealthy foods at the top that you eat sparingly. Your goal is to have a solid foundation of "Rising Stars, Stars, and Ambassadors" followed by a bulk of "It's a Paycheck" employees, followed by the least amount at the top of "I Don't Give a Shit" employees.

---

11   Valéne Jouany and Mia Mäkipää, "8 Employee Engagement Statistics You Need to Know in 2021," smarp.com, January 4, 2021, https://blog.smarp.com/employee-engagement-8-statistics-you-need-to-know.

Rising Stars, Stars, and Brand Ambassadors (Engaged Employees): Loyal, emotionally committed to the mission and vision, aligned with organizational values. These will be the next generation of leaders and remain with the organization longer than anyone else.

It's a Paycheck (Unengaged Employees): Harder to identify, as they may be content in their role but do the bare minimum and are not fully committed to the mission, vision, values, or goals. Generally concerned about productivity in terms of how it impacts them and their paycheck but can still be transformed into "Rising Stars" through deeper understanding and mentoring.

I Don't Give a Shit (Actively Disengaged Employees): Consistently negative, heart of toxic environment, vocal about their unhappiness. Typically have a know-it-all attitude and think they should be in charge. Unproductive in their use of time to the point of having a significant negative influence over others.

A recent poll by Gallup found that 36 percent of employees were actively engaged (Rising Stars), 14 percent were actively disengaged (Don't Give a Crap), which leaves 50 percent somewhere in the middle (Paycheck).[12] As a leader, you should strive to move your workforce from the middle section to the bottom, meaning you identified individuals who did not fully understand the mission, vision, values and goals, but you educated and nurtured them.

ENGAGEMENT/ PRODUCTIVITY EXERCISE

So now that you have seen the three types of employees, how can you improve upon engagement and productivity within your team or

---

12   Jim Harter, "U.S. Employee Engagement Reverts Back to Pre-COVID-19 Levels," Gallup, October 16, 2020, https://www.gallup.com/workplace/321965/employee-engagement-reverts-back-pre-covid-levels.aspx.

organization? First, which classification of employee do you fall into? Second, do you currently have these individuals on your team or in your organization? And lastly, what are you doing about it?

What does a well-engaged and productive workforce look like? Ideally, many would say, "Give me a team or organization filled with Stars and Ambassadors," but come on … that is not realistic, nor should you waste your time trying to achieve that. But there is a model that you can follow that will help guide you toward assessing and understanding the level of engagement for yourself, your team, and your organization.

I have found the following questions are a great start to assessing and understanding where you stand in terms of engagement:

1. Do you or does your team/workforce know what is expected of you/them? Is there clarity on what the end product is that's being produced and *why* it's being produced?

2. Do you or your team/organization have the resources, training, and opportunities to not only do the job but also grow personally and professionally?

3. Do you or your team/workforce receive recognition, appreciation, and feedback (both wins and opportunities for improvement) on a regular basis?

4. (A) Do you have the trust of your board of directors, knowing they have your best interests in mind? (B) Does your team/workforce have your trust in knowing you have their best interests in mind?

5. (A) Are you able to have your voice heard? (B) Is your team/workforce able to have their voices heard?

For yourself, I would ask you to give yourself a productivity score based on the Steps Scale from 0–10 with zero representing the least amount of productivity or engagement for each of the above questions using Part A for questions 4 and 5.

Once you've done that, you can score 0–10 for your team/workforce for each question using Part B for questions 4 and 5. Compare the two and see how your level of productivity/engagement aligns with the level of productivity/engagement for your team/workforce.

Maybe have other members of your leadership team go through the same exercise and see where there is agreement and disagreement in your perceptions. As a final step, add your score of engagement/productivity to that of the score for your team/workplace. A perfect score will be 100. So where do you land? Do you and your team earn an A? If not, you can isolate where the lowest scores and widest disparities of engagement/productivity lie and home in on improving those areas for yourself and your team.

SELF-ASSESSMENT

As we wrap up this last part of Personal GDP, it's important to remember the sequential order of the pyramid. Building from the bottom up, you start with Natural Resources as the foundation, followed by Health and Infrastructure, Human Capital, and Technology. If you address each of those effectively, then you will reach Productivity and ultimate economic and personal fulfillment, setting yourself up for the measurements of the Personal Happiness Index.

	1. I MEASURE MY DAY IN TERMS OF QUALITY, NOT QUANTITY.
2	I value each day based on what was accomplished and the impact of my actions rather than just counting tasks.
1	I am good at prioritizing my day based on what tasks have the most impact, but I can't help but feel a bit disappointed if the day doesn't go the way I planned.
0	My task list is my preferred method of judging my productivity, but I try to give some thought to the level of impact.
-1	I have trouble prioritizing items and get derailed by any unexpected event. I'm disappointed if I don't get through my task list.
-2	My agenda comes first, and I view all tasks equally. If I don't get them all done, then the day was a failure.

Not all tasks are created equal, and they should be prioritized by greatest impact. It can be a real challenge to shake off the task list mentality, I know … but your impact will last far longer than the "to do" list. It will end up in the wastebasket, but the quality actions you take each day to serve others will last a lifetime.

	2. MY DAY IS FILLED WITH MORE PROACTIVE THAN REACTIVE TASKS.
2	I look ahead based on long-term vision and goals, including leaving space in my schedule for the fires I will need to put out.
1	My tasks tend to be a mix of proactive and reactive, and I am working toward ensuring that I am not in constant "crisis mode."
0	I can't say whether I'm proactive or reactive—I just deal with things as they come up.
-1	I feel like most of my work has to be reactive because I'm constantly faced with new emergencies that have to be dealt with right away.
-2	I'm completely reactive and feel like I work crisis to crisis. I can't plan ahead for tomorrow because I'm still dealing with yesterday's problems.

To some degree, most of us like to feel needed by others. The downside of this is when we lose focus on the things we need to do because we are reacting to the fires and urgent requests coming from others. Not every request is going to be as urgent as the requester believes it to be. Being proactive in a strategy on how you choose your tasks can help you better assess whether the emergency is Defcon 5 (not urgent) or Defcon 1 (the world's about to end if you don't do something). The only way to get out of a constant state of crisis is to accept that crises will occur and to plan ahead.

3. AT THE END OF THE DAY, MY WORK ENERGIZES ME MORE THAN IT DRAINS ME, BOTH MENTALLY AND PHYSICALLY.

2	Even on really difficult days, I'm able to identify the good that came out of it. I feel invigorated by my work because I love what I do.
1	I'm regularly energized by the work I do at least three out of five days.
0	My energy level at the end of the day is purely based on what kind of day I had, good or bad.
-1	I leave work feeling drained most days and just glad that another day is over.
-2	Not only am I drained by my work, but I look for reasons to escape it whenever I can.

As I discussed before, loving what you do doesn't mean hard days won't happen. It just means that they don't leave you crushed. If you start your day mentally and physically drained, you can bet productivity will not be anywhere on the radar, no matter what your plan for the day happens to be.

	4. I'M INVESTED IN THE VISION, GOALS, MISSION, AND VALUES OF THE ORGANIZATION AND LOOK FOR WAYS TO ACTIVELY CONTRIBUTE AND MAKE A DIFFERENCE.
2	I am a "Super Star" employee. I'm totally bought into the mission and bring my best every day because I love what I do.
1	I'm somewhere between "Super Star" and "Paycheck" employee, but I'm headed the right direction.
0	I'm a "Paycheck" Employee—I don't dislike the work and do what I need to, but I don't actively think about the mission or how I can make a greater impact.
-1	I'm somewhere between being a "Paycheck" and "Don't Give a Crap" employee. I'm easily influenced by the attitude of others around me.
-2	I don't give a crap. Maybe I would if I was in a different position or being paid more, but I don't really think anyone would pay attention if I tried harder.

If you rank low on this one, that should be a good indicator to take a hard look at what you're passionate about and what you love. What changes do you need to make? Do you need to change your perspective? Or do you need to change organizations?

	5. I CAN CLEARLY IDENTIFY HOW MY NATURAL RESOURCES, HEALTH AND INFRASTRUCTURE, HUMAN CAPITAL, AND TECHNOLOGY (HUMAN TOUCH) CONTRIBUTE TO MY LEVEL OF PRODUCTIVITY.
2	Going back to my scores in the other assessments, I can clearly see a pattern in how my strengths—or weaknesses—in the other layers of P-GDP impact my level of Productivity.
1	I see a fair correlation between the other layers and Productivity, but I can also see where some improvements in those other areas could help me increase Productivity.
0	I see some correlation between the other layers and my level of Productivity, but I'm not sure yet how to best address the gaps I see.
-1	Overall, I'm not certain how improvements in the other P-GDP layers will make me more productive or fulfilled in my current work.
-2	I feel completely lost on the connections between my scores on the other layers of P-GDP and my Productivity.

Hopefully by this point, you can see some correlations between your measurements and how they impact one another. For example, you may score high in some areas, like knowing your Natural Resources, but perhaps you are in a workplace where you truly don't have the opportunity to put them to use, which affects your level of engagement and overall productivity. The clearer picture you have on how your scores impact your Productivity, the clearer the path you need to take to a more productive and fulfilled work life.

CONCLUSION

Too often, leaders either overlook or honestly just don't care about their team or organization as long as they are producing and maintaining a level of profitability. But as soon as the profits begin to slide or the quality of the product declines, the first thing they do is make cuts or reduce their expenses. How many leaders pause and ask themselves, "Could this decline be attributed to an unengaged workforce? Is it possible that the cause of these unfavorable results is due to lack of appreciation or opportunity within my organization or team? Should I take the time to meet with the workforce and understand what can be improved upon or eliminated due to waste?"

Those are the questions an engaged leader thinks about, but a disengaged or disconnected or self-centered leader would never have that cross their mind. In that case, you have an "I Don't Give a Crap" leader ... which is another dilemma completely.

To take this back to Human Capital and quality over quantity,

The clearer picture you have on how your scores impact your Productivity, the clearer the path you need to take to a more productive and fulfilled work life.

I would rather work short staffed with a small team of exceptional individuals than fully staffed with a team filled with mediocrity. When *it* hits the fan, true leadership is never just about your efforts and know-how, but the team behind you.

Hopefully, this walk through Personal GDP has given you some insight into how you can better position yourself to face adversity and choose the right hard that separates leadership from leadershi*. On the following page, you'll tally up your scores to get a cumulative score for P-GDP, but it's only half of the picture. Ready to fill in the other half?

PERSONAL GDP SCORE

Now, take a moment to add up all of your scores from chapters 2 through 6 and you'll have your total Personal GDP. Depending on the number, you'll know which "bucket" of development you're in:

INSTRUCTIONAL LEAGUE: -50 TO 0

Yes, you have work to do, but you're in the game and now you've got a clearer, honest picture of where you are and where you need to be. Don't give up! The opportunity for growth is a good thing.

MINOR LEAGUE: -0 TO +34

You're in the middle, and that's honestly not a bad place to be. You can harness your strengths to make improvements in your weaker areas, and now you've got a better sense of how to choose your hard and inspire greatness.

MAJOR LEAGUE: +35 TO +50

Congrats! You're on your way to being a P-GDP guru. But don't stop. In your state of thriving, your challenge is to sustain that level and look for ways to inspire and influence others too.

PART 3
PERSONAL HAPPINESS INDEX

SOCIAL SUPPORT

Remember, no man is a failure who has friends.
- FROM IT'S A WONDERFUL LIFE,
DIRECTED BY FRANK CAPRA

Recently, my son came up to work to have lunch with me and tell me about a debate that happened in his international business class just that morning.

"The professor was talking about the value of GDP and the Happiness Index," he said, "and he asked us which one is a better measure of the prosperity and success of a nation."

He went on to say that in true American tradition, the class was divided in the ensuing debate: some declared GDP the best, others were adamant about the Happiness Index, and then there were even some who thought maybe it was some mixture of each, like picking from a buffet.

Of course, at this point in the book, you should know that not only do I think that it's a mixture of each, but that it's the *combina-*

tion of the two. Looking at Personal GDP is extremely helpful but incomplete in measuring your success. You have to add in Personal Happiness to have a more rounded perspective, especially if we believe in Cody Bellinger's quote about success coming from happiness.

Now, I know the "pursuit of happiness" can feel elusive, as though it's something you can chase but never completely get—like Charlie Brown trying to kick the football Lucy is always yanking out from under him. But to remind you of what I said *way* back in the first chapter, it's important to see happiness as different from joy. Where joy can be found in a moment—earning that bonus at work, proposing to your significant other, your kid's face on Christmas morning—happiness is a long-term state of being.

Before you call me a liar and heretic, I'm not saying that hard days won't happen or that life won't throw you a curveball. It will. But it means that you've got some tools in place to help you keep pursuing that happiness no matter what comes your way. This is why Social Support is not only critical in that pursuit, but it also forms the base within Vizzoca's Hierarchy of Needs for the Personal Happiness Index in the same way Natural Resources formed the base for Personal GDP.

PERSONAL SOCIAL SUPPORT

Think about it this way: nations need to build alliances with one another not just for financial gain, but for security purposes, for regional interests, and for promoting peace and national well-being. This happens through sending ambassadors and even international sporting events like the Olympic and Paralympic Games.

In the 2020 World Happiness Report, which ranked the happiness index for 153 nations, it's almost as beneficial to look at the lowest ranking members of the report as it is to look at the highest ranking.

In fact, it's not surprising that one nation in the bottom five even showed an almost nonexistent level of Social Support.

Now, Social Support within a nation can exist on multiple levels. For example, you can take a country like Colombia (#44 on the 2020 report), which does not perform so well in regards to *international* Social Support but has a very strong *internal* Social Support when you look at the community and family structures that are in place *within* the country.

It's the same with people. We need a diversification of support on multiple levels. You need support at work, sure, but you need it outside of work too.

In my efforts to diversify my own social support, I've made it a point to be "responsibly social" with people from work. If a gathering is happening and I'm invited, sure, I'll make an appearance because I want to be approachable—but I'll always appear with my wife there, and I won't drink so that I don't end up as the guy with the tie wrapped around his head dancing on

We need a diversification of support on multiple levels. You need support at work, sure, but you need it outside of work too.

the table. I don't need my kids—or anyone really—stumbling across that on YouTube.

In fact, I was previously part of a growing healthcare organization where we worked long hours and everyone there worked really hard. During one holiday season, one particular division leader decided to throw a huge holiday celebration at a local bar/restaurant, inviting all his staff, around 150 in total. Now, he wanted to not only show his appreciation but that he was also "one of the guys." And that's where he made a costly mistake.

As the celebration came to a close, someone suggested a group picture to commemorate the occasion, so everyone left gathered together with him in the very center. Little did he know that this picture would be the beginning of the end of not only his career but his family.

Several days later, he was served with a lawsuit and a human resources case against him for sexual harassment as one of his staff members accused him of inappropriate touching during the photograph. He was suspended pending investigation—which took almost a year—and not only was he terminated for zero tolerance, but his wife left and divorced him.

The irony of this was that he ended up winning his case when his accuser admitted to setting him up. He received monetary damages, sure, but the real damage was done, and he had lost his family and everything he had worked for. More than anything, this taught me that leaders need to act like leaders—*always*.

QUALITY OVER QUANTITY

Let's face it. Leadership means you are at the top of the food chain, the influencer, but you've also got the biggest target on your back. As the saying goes, "the higher they are, the harder they fall."

Leadership is a lonely business, and the higher you rise, the lonelier it gets. At the same time, it gets busier as more people want to be around you or get time on your calendar. I've had to ask myself over time, "Do these people actually want to be around me because they care about me? Or are they just trying to stroke my ego to advance their own careers and agenda?"

Just like we discussed with Productivity, Social Support should be focused on quality over quantity. Loneliness is a feeling, not a scientific measurement of how often you are by yourself, so it's possible to be constantly surrounded by people and still feel lonely.

So Social Support isn't about the quantity of people around you, but the *quality* of people around you, and the depth of the relationships you have with them. As I see it, there are four vitally critical elements that determine the quality of relationships you build:

- You have to have **Trust.**
- You have to have **Honesty.**
- You have to be comfortable with showing **Vulnerability** at times, without fear of judgment.
- And you should get a measure of **Joy** from the relationship.

SOCIAL SUPPORT PODS

Establishing a strong Social Support Network starts by clearly understanding that there is not just one network but multiple **Support Pods** within your network. There are many types of Support Pods, but I'll highlight a few that I've found to be essential:

Family Support Pod

Workplace Support Pod

Friend Support Pod

Peer, or Business, Support Pod

Each one has varying degrees of trust, honesty, vulnerability, and joy, but be careful … there are traps in each also. Just like you shouldn't hand out your own trust, honesty, and vulnerability to just anyone, neither should you be quick to accept it from just anyone. Establishing these pods helps you set up boundaries.

Think of each pod as a bullseye where the highest level of trust, honesty, vulnerability, and joy occurs within the inner circle, the center of the bullseye as illustrated in the **Social Support Bullseye** diagram:

SOCIAL SUPPORT BULLSEYE

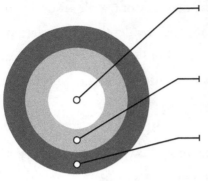

INNER CIRCLE (CORE):
This is the area in which the most trust, honesty, and vulnerability that can be displayed without the fear of judgement. This is reserved for special people of the three pods.

PRIMARY CIRCLE:
This is where you can speak with transparency and, although trust and honesty are critical, vulnerability happens infrequently.

SECONDARY CIRCLE:
Although this group is furthest from the core, it is vital in terms of having a network that you can lean on in unexpected times. This group may someday move towards your core.

FAMILY POD

This is the most important pod for me, maybe because I'm Italian, but I would not have it any other way. (No *Godfather* jokes, all right? I've heard them all.) Not everyone in my large family is in the inner circle, but I have the ability to let them into the **Inner Circle** from the **Primary Circle**.

A few years back, I listened to an interview with the former CEO of Pepsi, Indra Nooyi, in which she described a moment when she returned home from a stressful day. Her mother was living with her at the time, and as she entered her house, she started to tell the story of her day.

After a couple of minutes of ranting, her mother stopped her and asked, "Did you bring home the milk I asked you to get this morning?"

Surprised, Indra responded with "Are you hearing the story of my day?"

And without missing a beat, her mother answered, "You may be the CEO of Pepsi, but once you enter this house, you are a wife, mother, and daughter ... and we need milk."

I love that story because it's a reminder to all of us not to be the CEO or manager with your **Family Pod**, but to just be *you*, not because that's what they expect, but it's what they want and need.

Over time, you'll experience ebb and flow with who is in each circle. There's a fine line in the Family Pod between the Inner and Primary Circles because there will be times where you can call on the "reserves" from the Primary Circle for additional support to help you get through tougher times or when you need that extra validation.

For example, my parents and sisters mean the world to me, but as a leader in the midst of the pandemic, I didn't want to burden them with the challenges, criticism, or negativity that I was facing. My wife and kids were all I needed in my Inner Circle in that season; they were my escape, my de-stressors. But when I was battling cancer, I needed everyone who was in my Inner and Primary Circles, and even the **Secondary Circle** most days.

You may be wondering, "Then who is in the Secondary Circle?" Well, I think of my Secondary Circle as individuals whom I seldom see, but their support is there as occasion arises. They might be the family you only see at reunions or special occasions but are "on call" when you need them. It could be the accountant cousin you need to run a question by or the retired mechanic uncle you call to see if the repair quote you received sounds fair. They fill in the niche needs you have that your Inner and Primary groups may not be able to meet in special circumstances.

As one of my favorite (top three for sure) artists, John Mellencamp, once said—I mean, sang: "Life is short, even in its longest day." I remind myself and my team about this all the time so I don't forget what's important … family.

WORKPLACE POD

When you work at the same place with the same people for a long time, you're going to get close to them—for better or worse. After all, most of us will spend more time with our "work family" than we will our real families, so it will be natural to get really close to some of your coworkers. As I mentioned earlier, I think it's wise to draw clear boundaries between you and those who report to you, both for your protection and theirs. At the same time, it's perfectly okay—and encouraged—to have a select group of peers that can form your **Workplace Pod**.

As a leader, I have created an Inner Circle in my organization that consists of a small group of colleagues. These are individuals I can trust, be very honest with, and where vulnerability exists but occurs in a slightly different manner than it does with the Family Pod. Now, this doesn't develop overnight. In fact, it took me four years to build a tight Inner Circle within my C-Suite.

Your professional Primary Circle should be made up of some individuals that can be brought into the Inner Circle on a project-by-project basis. And the Secondary Circle should be individuals a little further from the Primary Circle but still very valuable to the team. But unlike with the Family Pod, you can recruit new members—or release them—in your Workplace Pod. These could also be individuals identified as candidates for leadership training programs (such as our employee recognition program) who have the capacity to grow into trusted, honest leaders within the organization.

There are two extremes a leader should be especially cautious of in this pod. On one end, there is the manager who has no relationships whatsoever with their team members and views everyone as a replaceable being—a transaction, if you will. On the other end, there is the manager who wants so much to be "one of the guys" that they have allowed the lines between work and social life to blur and cross over, setting the stage for both personal and professional confusion. Instead, we should strive to be leaders who have deep relationships but clearly understand the boundaries between work and social life and can keep them separated in such a way that will actually benefit everybody.

FRIEND POD

Every leader needs a pod that allows them to escape the world of the politics and stress of work. This is a pod where work is not discussed but instead should include topics like your kids, spouse or partner, sports, movies, and other common interests—as long as they're legal ones.

A **Friend Pod** Inner Circle is often small but very powerful and therapeutic in that it can be an escape from the day-to-day, allowing you to laugh and decompress. Now, I intentionally keep a small number of friends in my Inner Circle because, well, that's just me. I have a few friends that I can have a beer with and just laugh about anything. Think of this Inner Circle as your "safe zone" where you can say anything without the fear of judgment or ridicule and where you can give and receive honest and thoughtful feedback since these are your true friends.

I think by now you understand the concept of having a Primary and Secondary Circle, and the rules are the same here. And remember, you get to choose these individuals to be in your circles, so you can trade or release them as needed. Geography, life stages, and obligations may determine who is in which circle, but the point is that they are there.

For example, a few years back, I became friends with a former NFL quarterback. When we first started hanging out, he would ask me about business, and I would say, "I don't want to talk about business."

Then I'd want to talk about football, and he'd say, "I don't want to talk about football."

So we came to an agreement. We wouldn't talk about business or football but just stick to life. And that's the great thing about the Friend Support Pod: you have an opportunity to really diversify your support network and unplug from the topics that fill your workdays.

PEER POD

The **Peer Pod** can prove a pitfall for some leaders since only a peer in your industry or in your position can understand the pressures and challenges that come with leadership. In many instances, it's reaffirming to hear, "Yes, I understand exactly what you're going through," but ultimately your Peer Pod is based upon sharing a commonality.

I'm on the board of directors of a local healthcare council and am the lone representative of senior care among mostly hospital and health system executives. I decided to reach out to the CEO of the council with a request: could we convene the leaders of the other faith-based organizations within the region for one hour a week to share our challenges?

He agreed, and I'll be honest … the first meeting was very quiet. The awkward kind of quiet—you know what I mean. Although people were receptive to the idea, they were a bit skeptical about opening up, and I did much of the talking, reminding everyone that we were all here for one another. But by the fourth meeting, our group had started to experience individual COVID-19 outbreaks, and we all came together, sharing PPE and testing supplies, and my organization even took on some of their patients to share the burden.

Within this Peer Pod, I've identified leaders I consider in my Inner Circle, those I can call or email and meet for coffee to run ideas by to get another perspective and vice-versa. Some might be tempted to believe it's unwise to share info with a peer if they are technically a competitor, but again, you get to choose who you invite into those circles and who you trust.

EXERCISE: PLOTTING YOUR PODS

Before we head into the self-assessment, I think it could be important to go through the exercise of plotting out your pods. You should start with the ones already listed here: Family, Workplace, Friends, Peers; but you may have other pods to add to the group. You might add in a **Faith Pod** if that is an important aspect of your life, or a Health Pod if that is something that will help you increase your score from Health and Infrastructure.

Now, it's okay for there to be some overlap—in fact, there *should* be overlap. For example, I consider my wife as part of both my Family and Friend Pod Inner Circles because we are friends first and foremost. Maybe you have a family member that works alongside you, placing them in both your Family and Workplace Pods. In those cases, you get a two-for-one deal.

Three things you should learn from this exercise:

What are your established pods? Which ones do you need to add?

Who is in each pod, especially the three circles of each?

Whose pods are *you* in? Can your pods help you identify where you can be a part of someone else's Social Support?

SELF-ASSESSMENT

Hopefully, the exercise above will help you have a clearer picture of who makes up your Social Support Network. If you've got a lot of blank spots, then you already know you've got more work to do, but now it's time to compare that to the questions below so you can figure out the direction you need to take.

1. I CAN CLEARLY IDENTIFY PEOPLE FOR MY INNER, PRIMARY, AND SECONDARY CIRCLES FOR MY FAMILY POD.	
2	Not only can I identify those individuals, but I would say that I have strong relationships with them built on trust, honesty, vulnerability, and joy.
1	I can identify multiple individuals in my Secondary and Primary Circles and at least one individual in my Inner Circle.
0	I can identify some people in my Secondary and Primary Circles, but I'm not sure I trust anyone enough to be in my Inner Circle.
-1	I can place family members in my Secondary Circle, but I'm not sure who I trust enough to be in a Primary or Inner Circle.
-2	I'm not sure I have enough trust, honesty, or vulnerability with anyone in my family to qualify them for any circles.

Remember, placing people in your circles isn't just about assigning them based on proximity or how closely related you are but about the level of trust, honesty, vulnerability, and joy you have with them. For example, it's possible you could have a cousin in your Inner Circle but perhaps a sibling in your Secondary Circle if the level of trust and honesty you have with them is lower. And let's face it, most of us have that one family member we wish we could move to someone else's pod ...

	2. I CAN CLEARLY IDENTIFY PEOPLE FOR MY INNER, PRIMARY, AND SECONDARY CIRCLES FOR MY WORK POD.
2	Not only can I identify those individuals, but I would say that I have strong relationships with them built on trust, honesty, vulnerability, and joy.
1	I can identify multiple individuals in my Secondary and Primary Circles and at least one individual in my Inner Circle.
0	I can identify some people in my Secondary and Primary Circles, but I'm not sure I trust anyone enough to be in my Inner Circle.
-1	I can place family members in my Secondary Circle, but I'm not sure who I trust enough to be in a Primary or Inner Circle.
-2	I'm not sure I have enough trust, honesty, or vulnerability with anyone in my workplace to qualify them for any circles.

Are these almost exactly the same as the qualifications for the Family Pod? Yes. Is that on purpose? Yes! Obviously, the type of honesty, trust, vulnerability, and joy present within the workplace is a different brand than that in the Family Pod, but they still have to be present for you to effectively identify individuals for each of the circles.

3. I CAN CLEARLY IDENTIFY PEOPLE FOR MY INNER, PRIMARY, AND SECONDARY CIRCLES FOR MY FRIEND POD.

2	Not only can I identify those individuals, but I would say that I have strong relationships with them built on trust, honesty, vulnerability, and joy.
1	I can identify multiple individuals in my Secondary and Primary Circles and at least one individual in my Inner Circle.
0	I can identify some people in my Secondary and Primary Circles, but I'm not sure I trust anyone enough to be in my Inner Circle.
-1	I can place family members in my Secondary Circle, but I'm not sure who I trust enough to be in a Primary or Inner Circle.
-2	I'm not sure I have enough trust, honesty, or vulnerability with any of my friends to qualify them for any circles.

You might have found during the Plotting Your Pods exercise that you have multiple Friend Pods based on different social structures in your life. In general, there's absolutely nothing wrong with that, but I think it's important to zero in on specific friends with whom you have the highest level of honesty, trust, vulnerability, and joy.

4. I CAN CLEARLY IDENTIFY PEOPLE FOR MY INNER, PRIMARY, AND SECONDARY CIRCLES FOR MY PEER POD.

2	Not only can I identify those individuals, but I would say that I have strong relationships with them built on trust, honesty, vulnerability, and joy.
1	I can identify multiple individuals in my Secondary and Primary Circles and at least one individual in my Inner Circle.
0	I can identify some people in my Secondary and Primary Circles, but I'm not sure I trust anyone enough to be in my Inner Circle.
-1	I can place family members in my Secondary Circle, but I'm not sure who I trust enough to be in a Primary or Inner Circle.
-2	I'm not sure I have enough trust, honesty, or vulnerability with any of my peers to qualify them for any circles.

I'll admit it … this one can be really, really tricky to figure out. And it's okay if you find you have a lot of blank spots to fill in. But if you score well in some of the other pods and low here, then that should bring some clarity for you to be on the lookout for possible peers. You can't find them if you don't look for them!

	5. I HAVE A DEEP UNDERSTANDING OF HOW I CONTRIBUTE TO THE SOCIAL SUPPORT OF OTHERS IN MY LIFE.
2	Not only do I think about those who are a part of my Social Support Network, but I actively think of how I can be a part of their Social Support Pods.
1	I have a fair idea of the people within my Social Support Network I can also be a support to.
0	I'm not proactive about who I can be a support for, but I sometimes support others as occasions arise.
-1	I haven't given much thought to how I can support others on an active basis and tend to mostly think of what I get from others.
-2	I don't feel supported by others, so I don't see why I should look to support them.

A final thought for our modern world … your Social Support Network is not the same as your social media network. Maybe I should've said this earlier, but this is where you have to go back to quality over quantity. You may have one hundred thousand followers on social media, but you can't honestly say you have a level of honesty, trust, and vulnerability with all of those people—and certainly the dopamine hit you get from social media notifications doesn't equate to the joy and happiness you can receive from a real relationship.

The dopamine hit you get from social media notifications doesn't equate to the joy and happiness you can receive from a real relationship.

CONCLUSION

As we move higher up Vizzoca's Hierarchy of Needs for the Personal Happiness Index, you'll quickly see how essential it is to have a strong and clearly defined Social Support Network. In fact, it will be difficult to move forward without establishing your pods and their corresponding circles.

To tweak the opening quote, I'd say that "No man is a failure who has social support." As you navigate the hard things that life throws at you, your Social Support will be key in getting through the hard and finding your great. People who do great things are often surrounded by great people.

Sure, you may fail on certain days, and you'll make mistakes along the way, but you won't ever be a failure if you've got people you can count on to care for you through those moments. As we get into Positive and Negative Affect in the following chapters, we're going to turn the lens outward and take a hard look at how you impact not just your Social Support Network but everyone you come into contact with.

CHAPTER 8

POSITIVE AFFECT

Once you replace negative thoughts with positive
ones, you'll start having positive results.
— *WILLIE NELSON*

I'll never forget sitting in a doctor's office between my parents when he came in to announce that I had cancer and the look of fear filling my parents' eyes. But I'll also never forget the next words out of the doctor's mouth: "Look, if you're going to get cancer, this is the best one to get."

And in a moment, he pivoted the conversation away from panic … to putting a plan in place for what we needed to do to fight back and win.

Even though there was a plan in place, it wasn't always smooth sailing. Some of those chemo sessions went really sideways, yet the doctors and nurses were always so positive, letting me know that I was a fighter … even when I didn't always feel like one.

This is deeper than just "bedside manner." You can't control everything that happens to you, but you *can* control your response.

As a leader, you're going to face crises every day, and you can greet it with either panic or a plan. It's all about your affect ... and the effect it brings out of people.

Without getting too grammatical, it's really easy to mix up the words "affect" and "effect." It's okay to admit it. I've done it too—but at least I can blame that on English being my second language. After all, they sound a lot alike, and both can be used as a verb or a noun. While they are different in meaning, there is a clear correlation between them.

The way I like to think of it is this: "affect" is the cause and "effect" is the result.

From a leadership perspective, "affect" connotes the direct influence and impact you have on your team and organization. "Effect" is the resulting response brought about by that influence. "Affect" could be seen as the external presentation of your inner beliefs and drivers, that is, the qualities that others notice about you which make an impact on them. Got all that?

So, leaving grammar behind—you're welcome—and putting it back into terms of my cancer experience, it looks something like this:

THE AFFECT OF DOCTORS/NURSES:
Positive confidence and individualized concern as if I was their primary interest even though they had other patients.

THE EFFECT ON MY PARENTS:
As a result of the affect of the doctors and nurses, my parents felt calm and confident in the treatment process. My parents then exuded an affect of calm and positive support.

THE EFFECT ON ME:
My parents' affect made me the recipient of positivity and optimism, resulting in me feeling more positive and optimistic.

So in the same way, your affect will ultimately cascade down and have an effect on each layer of your team and organization. While you may not have control over certain situations, you will always have the control of how you will *affect* it. If you choose to create a culture of wellness and appreciation, the effect will be the outcome of that affect.

POSITIVE AFFECT

In the World Happiness Index, Positive Affect can be seen as how a nation is able to face a crisis and put a plan into place. Does the leadership of the country move the population into a positive direction of problem-solving? Or do they capitulate to chaos?

People look to leaders in the face of a crisis, and they expect leadership to set the tone and direction. With the Personal Happiness Index, it's the same. In the face of a negative situation, a

> **While you may not have control over certain situations, you will always have the control of how you will affect it.**

leader has a responsibility to their team to think about their affect and the resulting impact it will make. One's affect will permeate every decision that gets made during the course of the crisis.

For example, when the COVID-19 pandemic hit, we decided to restrict family visitations at our facilities to reduce the spread of the virus. Of course, this was a drastic change to the normal rules and freedoms for families and friends to visit their loved ones in our care, so you can imagine the immediate effect of that. It was extremely negative. It created a great deal of anxiety, uncertainty, and feelings of guilt and anger.

It wasn't easy being at the forefront of that decision, given the sometimes inappropriate (and very personal) rhetoric that followed. In fact, it would have been very easy to give in to the pressure of families, but I knew our response had to start with me, and I was determined to remain focused and stick to the plan even if it wasn't popular.

It's the difference between being an influencer and being influenced. As CEO, I was in the position to affect everyone—staff, residents, family, and even the public as media outlets reached out for interviews about our pandemic response. Given the magnitude of the crisis, I was all the more grateful for a strong Social Support Network that allowed me to escape the craziness. To remain the influencer rather than become influenced, you need that occasional escape to grant you not only a reprieve, but also a renewed perspective.

PRACTICED POSITIVITY

Now, I can already hear some of you protesting, "But I'm just not a naturally positive person." Well, I've got a confession to make—neither am I. I'm a pessimist and natural worrier. My mind tends to go to the worst possible outcome for a situation. I don't just see the glass as half empty—I assume the water in the glass has been contaminated.

No … for me, a positive affect is something I've had to practice. I worked in an environment previously where we seemed to constantly be in crisis mode. I'd get so anxious sitting in meetings that I'd have to leave the room just to give myself a break. I'd go into the bathroom and focus on my breathing, tuning out the negative thoughts and getting back to a place of calm.

Another good exercise I've learned is to think about past successes when I face a crisis. At that same company, I'd return to the meeting room and say, "Hey, remember how we got through X situation?" And suddenly the whole tone of the conversation would shift from "The end is nigh" to "We can do this!"

In addition to these practices, I also subscribe to some emails of encouraging anecdotes and quotes. No matter what's going on, I can open one of those emails and get into a better, more positive headspace.

And when all else fails, one of the great benefits of leading a faith-based nonprofit is that the occasional ninety-year-old Sister will pick up on my stress levels, take me by the elbow, and tell me, "You're not in control. Go back to your office, shut the door, and pray on it. There's already a plan … you just need to remain calm and carry it out."

So maybe you don't have a wise nun in your life like that, but again, that's why you need multiple Social Support Pods, people who will have a positive effect on you. Nobody likes to be around a negative person. As a leader, a Positive Affect will drive people toward you, thus creating a stronger support network. As I've said before, I want people to follow me not because they *have* to but because they *want* to.

THERMOSTAT VS. THERMOMETER

You've probably heard this analogy before—the idea of being a human thermostat, a person who sets the temperature, rather than being a thermometer, a person who only responds to the temperature around them.

Early on in the pandemic, it was decided that I should record a video message for the entire organization where I reiterated that "We will all practice focus, strength, and safety for ourselves and our residents."

Stay calm. Stay focused. Stay Positive. This became an anthem for our entire team from that moment forward.

I wanted to affect the morale of the organization and "set the temperature" with a message of optimism and a reminder that our ultimate goal was to keep everyone safe. As the pandemic went on, that message never wavered—and the effect was noticeable. The message became part of the infrastructure for the health of our organization as staff increased support for one another. Did we have some people who couldn't handle it? Absolutely. But what was the alternative? How many more staff would have crumbled if I had projected negativity and panic?

Gradually, my Positive Affect became the positive affect of the staff—and then transferred to our resident families as they realized we were truly committed to keeping their loved ones safe and protected.

It's no different for any leader in any organization. It's not an issue of personality or temperament but deciding whether you will be the thermostat or the thermometer. It's okay to feel emotions in the face of stress, and it's even okay to show them in appropriate ways … but that doesn't mean you have to be ruled by your emotions. There is an anonymous quote I love that I think perfectly captures this idea: "Life is not happening to you; it is responding to you."

BROADEN AND BUILD

All right, we've discussed grammar and cancer … time for some psychology. Have you ever heard of the Broaden and Build Theory? It was first proposed by Barbara Frederickson and is associated with the subject of positive psychology, exploring the role that positive emotions play in building resiliency. The idea is that positive emotions (affect) can have the effect of broadening the awareness and response to situations as well as aid in building resiliency and skills necessary to address events that may arise in the future.

So let's apply this theory to the five measures of P-GDP to see how a leader's positive affect can influence or strengthen these areas. When P-GDP and P-HI are tied together, the Positive Affect a leader practices will allow them to take better advantage of both. Consider the following:

Natural Resources: A Positive Affect turns a leader to their natural strengths, talents, and resources to face a new challenge.

Health and Infrastructure: The positive leader engages in taking better care of their overall health and looks for ways to improve the health of others, lifting the mood and psyche for them and everyone around them.

Human Capital: A Positive Affect refocus on what improvements can be made to get through a negative situation and come out the other side of it stronger.

Technology: The positive leader understands that their human touch will be amplified and that their demeanor will have a direct impact on their team. Also, the positive leader will look to use High-Tech resources (i.e., my video message) to spread a Positive Affect among the team.

Productivity: A Positive Affect understands that no progress can be made wallowing in negativity. Rather, a positive affect will inspire a spirit of positive productivity, both in oneself and throughout the organization.

Like choosing your hard, you also have a choice in pursuing a Positive Affect. While there are many different types, I believe there are six that all leaders should have and build off of. You can think of these affects as your **CHOICE**:

CONFIDENCE

HOPE

OPTIMISM

INSPIRATION

CALM

ENGAGEMENT

Since I'm not a psychologist, I'm going to borrow someone else's degree for a moment to encourage you in practicing the Broaden and Build Theory. When pursuing these affects, it's important to understand that positive emotions are not just ones you experience as a reaction, but they are also feelings that you can willingly call up as needed.

POSITIVE EFFECTS FROM POSITIVE EMOTIONS

Enhances long-term sense survival by giving you greater coping resources.

Increases your creativity by allowing you to step out of survival mode to consider more options.

Enables you to see the big picture by stepping out of survival mode and thinking more clearly.

Improves your psychological resilience by giving you more tools to manage negative emotions.

Allows you to flourish rather than just survive (i.e., live the life of your dreams rather than just avoid the life of your nightmares).

Puts negative emotions into broader context of the big picture, helping you to see that the current situation is not your destiny and that things can change for the better in the future.

Gives greater meaning to life so that you can find the "good in the bad," including making it easier to see positivity in future situations by recognizing that things change and that you can always find some positive in a negative situation.

Increases feelings of well-being that improve in a positive upward cycle, including the ability to bounce back in the face of new obstacles.

Helps you see yourself as "wise" so you can operate from your "wise" mind rather than reacting out of negative emotion.

Greater social integration as you move in an upward cycle.

Greater distress tolerance aids in the ability to react calmly in the face of distress.

Better emotion regulation aids the ability to manage your negative emotions.

Increased job satisfaction, especially if you experience positive emotions at work.

Improved work performance in your job or career by giving you tools to improve your work and face obstacles with clarity.

Source: Arlin Cuncic. "An Overview of Broaden and Build Theory." VeryWellMind.com. December 22, 2020.

Since I'm not a naturally positive person, I've had to seek out some ways to "broaden and build" my Positive Affect to have a practical impact on my team. Thankfully, it's not rocket science, and you can do all of these things no matter what line of work you're in:

1. Celebrate the wins—No matter how little, take the time to recognize and celebrate accomplishments of a team, person, or the organization as a whole.

2. Give praise and gratitude—Be grateful for the work of others and say, "Thank you." Those two words alone can change the whole trajectory of someone's day.

3. Engage in a hobby or activity as a diversion—This allows you to escape the day-to-day stress, clear your mind, rest, and reset.

4. Reflection—Look back on positive experiences and times of gratitude. Recalling past successes can become positivity fuel to refill your tank.

5. Create experiences—I, for one, would rather spend time and money on an experience than on material possessions. The memories created through experiences will last a lifetime from which you can generate a source of Positive Affect.

A few years back, a palliative care nurse named Bronnie Ware wrote a book called *Top Five Regrets of the Dying*. In it, she discusses that the fifth regret could be summarized as "I wish I had let myself be happier." In one conversation with a dying patient, she says, "We have the freedom to choose what we focus on. I try to choose the positive stuff."[13]

---

13 Bronnie Ware, *Top Five Regrets of the Dying: A Life Transformed by the Dearly Departing* (Carlsbad: Hay House, 2012), 210.

I sometimes will ask our residents what one thing they would do differently with their lives. I've yet to have one tell me, "I'd make more money," or "I wish I'd worked more." Instead, their answers to me center on this idea of allowing themselves to be happier by spending more time with their loved ones or pursuing a dream.

One of the great insights I took away from Ware's book is that focusing on the negative

> **Since happiness is a choice and positive affect is one of our determining factors in happiness, then it must also be seen as a choice.**

is a sure-fire way to fill your life with regrets. And since happiness is a choice and positive affect is one of our determining factors in happiness, then it must also be seen as a choice. And as a choice, it is one that you have the power to make and grow in.

SELF-ASSESSMENT

I can still sense some doubt—and dread—out there. Maybe you're in the camp that says, "Positivity doesn't guarantee a positive outcome." And you know what? You're right. But it sure doesn't hurt either, does it? It doesn't take a genius to see that a Positive Affect is way more likely to lead to a positive outcome or to understand the link between positivity and happiness.

	1. I CAN CELEBRATE THE WINS IN LIFE, NOT JUST FOR MYSELF BUT FOR OTHERS.
2	Not only do I celebrate the wins in the life of others, but I find success in the success of others.
1	When I see others succeed, I generally feel a sense of excitement for them and find encouragement in it.
0	I'm able to celebrate the wins of those I feel closest to because it typically means a win for me too.
-1	Unless there is a direct connection to helping me succeed, I have difficulty celebrating the wins of others.
-2	When I see others succeed, all I can see is my failures, and I become jealous.

It's all too common these days to compare ourselves to others, especially when social media encourages people to filter their lives by highlighting their wins. But instead of seeing the successes of others as some kind of threat or attack, a Positive Affect should find encouragement and motivation in the wins of others.

2. I REGULARLY LOOK FOR WAYS TO SHOW GRATITUDE TO OTHERS IN WORD AND DEED, MAKING SURE THEY UNDERSTAND THAT I TRULY MEAN IT.

2	I go out of my way to make sure people in my life know they are appreciated, regardless of whether I receive any gratitude in return.
1	I have a good habit of saying "thank you" to people, knowing that I would like people to do the same for me.
0	I say "thank you" to people but mostly because it's just good manners, not with any real intention.
-1	Frankly, life is just too busy for gratitude. It sounds nice, but I'm not really sure how it will help me be a better leader.
-2	I don't expect people to show gratitude to me for doing my job, so why should I go out of my way to do that for them?

Most of us were probably taught to say "thank you" and "please" as good manners, but that's not the same as actually meaning it. True gratitude should have a Low-Tech human touch to it that others will find encouraging and motivating.

3. I REGULARLY ENGAGE IN HOBBIES THAT I ENJOY TO HELP ME MAINTAIN A POSITIVE MINDSET AND DE-STRESS.

2	I take time every day to engage in a hobby that will allow me to take a mental break, and I encourage others to do the same.
1	I definitely have hobbies that help me de-stress, but I could do better at making sure I engage in them more regularly.
0	I have hobbies that I enjoy, but I know I need to do a better job of utilizing them.
-1	I used to have hobbies, but I feel like I will be more stressed if I spend time on them instead of taking care of things.
-2	Hobbies are a waste of time for me and others.

Hobbies and interests can very much be part of the infrastructure you utilize to exercise some self-care and ensure mental, physical, and spiritual health. And as we saw in the productivity chapter, enjoying a hobby during a break can actually make one more productive and—you guessed it—happier.

	4. I'M ABLE TO REFLECT BACK ON PAST EXPERIENCES TO HELP ME REGAIN POSITIVITY IN THE MIDST OF A CHALLENGE.
2	I regularly reflect on past challenges I've overcome as motivation to overcome current challenges and encourage others to do the same.
1	I'm able to quickly recall past positive experiences to get back on track in the face of a negative experience.
0	I usually have to be reminded by someone else of a challenge I overcame before I'm able to feel better about my current situation.
-1	I'm aware that I have positive experiences, but I struggle to connect those to current problems or find any encouragement in them.
-2	The past is the past, and I don't see how spending time recalling it can help me with present challenges.

Remember in the productivity chapter when we discussed making a list of accomplishments? Well, now's the perfect time to pull them back out. There's nothing like a tangible reminder of past success to get the engine moving again and regain positive focus in the middle of a challenge.

5. I LOOK FOR WAYS TO CREATE EXPERIENCES BOTH FOR MYSELF AND OTHERS THAT WILL SERVE AS POSITIVE REINFORCEMENT FOR THE FUTURE.	
2	I'm actively thinking up ways to create positive experiences that will help me and those around me get through hard times.
1	I definitely see value in creating positive experiences for myself, but I need to work toward doing the same for others.
0	I certainly enjoy having positive experiences and see the benefit they provide, but I'm not actively engaged in creating any.
-1	I don't give much thought to creating experiences and struggle with seeing the benefit for myself and others.
-2	Creating positive experiences sounds nice, but I feel like it's more of a distraction from what I should be doing.

My kids can't tell you what I got them for Christmas five years ago. In fact, I probably couldn't tell you without pulling up an old bank statement. But they still talk about the time we went to the beach and how hard we laughed at the restaurant afterward. Experiences are directly tied to emotions and can be recalled at will. Likewise, creating positive experiences in the workplace can go a long way in boosting morale, increasing engagement, and retaining the best employees. Unless you *want* the worst employees for some reason …

CONCLUSION

Life will always throw you a negative situation in the form of an unruly customer, a complaining team member, a financial setback, a relationship problem … you fill in the blank. At the end of the day, positivity isn't about ignoring these facts of life but embracing the power that positivity can bring you in those moments.

Again, you don't need piles of research to see that positive people are happier people. And the truly great thing about positivity is that those who foster it and understand its potential don't want to keep it to themselves but want to share it with others. Give Positive Affect a try, and I can guarantee you'll start to see some positive effects.

CHAPTER 9
NEGATIVE AFFECT

Hoping for the best, prepared for the worst, and
unsurprised by anything in between.
— *MAYA ANGELOU*

In 2014, snowboarder Shaun White went to Sochi, Russia, with the goal of becoming the first Winter Olympian to win three consecutive gold medals in the same event—the half pipe. And there was no doubt about it; he was the man to beat.

But when the day of the final came, White had an uncharacteristic first run—full of falls, missed tricks, and being outperformed by younger snowboarders. While his second run was better, it wasn't enough to make up for the mistakes of the first run. Not only did he not win gold … he was nowhere on the podium as he landed in a disappointing fourth place. He was a good sport about it, taking ownership of his mistakes but still understandably crushed.

In an interview three years later, he spoke about that negative experience, saying, "It's like falling off a bike and you have the little scar from it—it's a part of you. It's something to learn from."[14]

I can completely empathize with his frustration, not because I've gotten fourth in snowboarding at the Olympics, but because when I was growing up, I was always taught that "second place is first loser." I know that sounds harsh nowadays, but back then, there was no such thing as a participation trophy. And I'm glad there wasn't because not winning the trophy was a negative that taught me to remember the feelings of sadness, rejection, and loss—and turn that into motivation.

Shaun White proved that sometimes a negative can be a good thing by reclaiming the gold medal at the PyeongChang Games. Given the choice, I'm sure he would still want to go back to Sochi and win the gold there too. But one could argue that his loss in Sochi gave him more drive to grow as an athlete in a way that winning might not have been able to do. I know it's a hypothetical, but one could imagine a scenario where a gold at Sochi would have led to a sense of complacency in his work and scaling back on training.

Tennis legend Jimmy Connors captured this mindset best when he said, "I hate to lose more than I love to win." While that may rub some people the wrong way, this positively negative attitude drove him to become the first man to hold the number one spot in tennis for more than two hundred weeks.

You have to look at Positive Affect and Negative Affect as a type of yin and yang that balance one another out. On the one hand, you don't want to be Pollyanna, seeing everything as rainbows and unicorns even when you've got a crisis staring you in the face. Nor do you want to be

---

14   *The Today Show*, "Shaun White: I've Never Gotten Over Finishing 4th in Sochi," NBC, February 8, 2017, https://www.youtube.com/watch?v=5M6ffF9Uiq4.

Eeyore and see doom and gloom in every little problem to the point that you just flop on the ground and don't even try.

Pessimism gets a bad rap, but it can be a good thing when it helps you be better prepared for crisis or conflict. For example, researcher Joseph Forgas found that those with a Negative Affect tend to be more cautious and that Negative Affect could also "improve a person's ability to detect deception."[15]

In military terms, you don't want a general who passively lets other countries invade our airspace saying, "Oh, I'm sure they're not going to attack. They're just coming by to wave and say hi." Hell no! You want the general that's going to get his best pilots up in the air and tell the interlopers to get their asses back on their side of the line.

Pessimism at its best is about caution and protection—being prepared for the worst because you take your role as a leader seriously. It's what you could call being "best-imistic"—fostering a healthy pessimism that helps you make the best decisions.

After all, there are different levels of negativity. It's one thing to be negative and analytical, where you consider the worst-case scenarios so you can take action—it's a whole other thing to be negative and an ass.

NEGATIVE AFFECT

In the World Happiness Index, Negative Affect is an experiential measure based on respondents reporting their emotions from the previous day— how many times they felt sad, worried, anxious, or generally pessimistic about their circumstances. From this, a score is derived to show the general level of emotional negativity present within a country.

---

15   Joseph Forgas, "Don't Worry, Be Sad! On the Cognitive, Motivational, and Interpersonal Benefits of Negative Mood," *Current Directions in Psychological Science* 22 (2013): 225–232.

Certainly, this same kind of gauge can be helpful in figuring out whether you are in the right role. If you're constantly miserable and anxious about your work, that's something you should pay attention to. But in the Personal Happiness Index, we are going to take a slightly different approach by looking at how harnessing a Negative Affect can work for your benefit as a leader.

One of the main instruments used to measure Negative Affect is PANAS (the Positive and Negative Affect Schedule), which is a scale that determines negative and positive affect based on ten items:

POSITIVE AFFECT	NEGATIVE AFFECT
Attentive	Hostile
Active	Irritable
Alert	Ashamed
Excited	Guilty
Enthusiastic	Distressed
Determined	Upset
Inspired	Scared
Proud	Afraid
Interested	Jittery
Strong	Nervous

Now, in the pursuit of balancing these two, you have to look at the positive aspects of the Negative Affect. For example, let's take hostility. Maybe you're wondering, "Nick, how the heck can that ever be a good thing?"

For me, hostility becomes a good thing when I need to protect my team. I've said it before—you can attack me all day long, but I'm not going to let you come after my staff. Period. Never hesitate to take one for your team or defend your team.

What about feelings like ashamed, guilty, and afraid? With these, I see the Negative Affect as a proactive approach to *avoid* these feelings. Because I've experienced shame, guilt, and fear at other times—both personally and professionally—I do whatever I can to avoid them.

In the same way Shaun White wanted to avoid the feeling of loss again and used that as motivation, leaders can do the same thing by using a cautious pessimism to succeed. Sometimes on the stairway to success, the journey is not just about doing the right things—it's also about *not* doing the wrong things.

> **Sometimes on the stairway to success, the journey is not just about doing the right things—it's also about not doing the wrong things.**

THE BATTLE AGAINST MEDIOCRITY

An excess of positivity—or "The Pollyanna Effect"—can lead to complacency and mediocrity, whereas Negative Affect can actually help protect from it. For example, my team knows that I'm a positive person 80–90 percent of the time, so when I'm off and my stress starts to show, they know something's wrong. They know it's serious and need to really pay attention and pick things up a notch. My staff knows now that when I say, "It's all good," that it's probably *not* all good.

Now, if your stress level is always set on high and every single task is a fire, then you're just dumping your negative psyche onto the team. I'm sure during World War II, there were plenty of times FDR sat back in his office with his face in his hands, thinking, "Holy cow ... how are we gonna get out of this one?" Because he knew the well-being of the country rested on his shoulders. But when he was making a speech, he couldn't be in a panic. "We have nothing to fear but fear itself," right?

Just like anything in life, moderation is key. Too much stress is a bad thing, yes, but the right amount of stress can help you approach problems with a sense of calculated risk and invite in trusted people to help you problem solve. And in this way, too, negative emotion can become a tool to push back against mediocrity in both your life and your organization as you harness it to become your best self.

One way to objectively look at problems is through asking the following questions:

WHAT DO WE KNOW?
WHAT DO WE STILL NEED TO KNOW?
WHAT DON'T WE KNOW?

You can also combine this with a typical SWOT analysis—looking at Strengths, Weaknesses, Opportunities, and Threats to determine:

WHERE ARE THE GAPS?
HOW DO WE FILL THEM?
WHAT DO WE NEED TO BE PURSUING AND PRIORITIZING?

The answers to these questions can help point you toward the specific questions you need to ask to break down the problem, remove panic from the crisis, and turn it into a solution. In the battle against mediocrity, you have to be just negative enough to look for the right problems to solve.

To go back to our organization's pandemic response, this is exactly what we were doing when we put together our clinical excellence team. We didn't know about COVID-19 when we first hatched the idea, but we were looking to answer those SWOT questions: What gaps did we need to fill? How? And what did our priorities need to be?

Once the news was breaking around the world, I was keeping up with it, including talking with family members in Italy, which was being slammed at the time. There was a lot we couldn't know yet, of course, but what we did know was that our residents would be the most vulnerable—and it was our job to protect them with everything we had.

As I've mentioned before, there were those who criticized our response and the preparations we were taking. They thought I was being unnecessarily negative, not to mention foolish for taking beds offline and affecting potential revenue. But by looking at the coming crisis through a negative affect, we were able to save ourselves a lot of *future* negativity. Our critics' failure to wield negative affect's potential left them scrambling and looking for direction once the surge hit.

INCREASING TRANSPARENCY

In fact, another positive of Negative Affect is increasing transparency. Sometimes when leaders want to keep things too outwardly positive, they make the mistake of covering up negative information. But Negative Affect has been shown in the same research I mentioned before to actually decrease this "misinformation effect." As a leader, your people need to know what is happening—good or bad—and if you withhold info that impacts everyone, then you're not being a good leader.

Now, you might argue and say, "I have to tell everyone everything? I need to drop off the bad quarterly report on everyone's desk?"

I'm not saying you have to go overboard, but if things are headed in the wrong direction, then your team needs to know so that changes can be made on an individual, team, and organizational level.

Just like how a Positive Affect gives you a **CHOICE** as discussed in the last chapter, a Negative Affect gives you a **CHANCE**:

CAUTIOUS
HARNESS
ANALYTICAL
NERVOUS
CALM
EQUIPPED

A bit about the word "harness"—it can be both a noun and a verb. As a noun, you could think of Negative Affect being a harness that helps you keep the right amount of tension to move things in the right direction, like a harness on a workhorse. As a verb, it's about empowerment and motivation, using that sense of pessimism to be more cautious and analytical.

Now, if you're paying close attention, you'll notice that I use calm as the second *C* in both CHOICE and CHANCE. That's because it's important to keep in perspective that both Positive and Negative Affect can keep you calm in the face of crisis and help you fight mediocrity.

When you're transparent with your team, projecting a sense of calm is key. You don't want to be honest at the risk of creating a panic and making everyone wet their pants. Instead, transparency should personalize the *why* for your team. I've been in jobs before where I was given tasks and the only reason given was "Because the CEO wants it done." That kind of BS is the same as when a parent tells their kid, "Do it because I said so." Even if the task gets done, where's the motivation behind it? Where's the drive to do it the best you can?

Instead, a transparent leader helps their team understand the reasons behind actions, even when there might be a bit of negativity mixed in. It helps them understand what the impact is to them as an individual, such as a bit of healthy fear of keeping their job, keeping the organization going—or in the case of my particular organization—saving lives.

Transparency also means making sure your team understands you and are on the same page as you. When I ask a staff member to do something and they say, "I heard you," I will often respond, "Hearing what I say is not the same as listening to what I say." That sounds negative, but I need to know they truly understand so we can avoid a negative situation if they misunderstood or are lacking in urgency.

Transparency, even when it hurts, can have some very positive long-term effects. It can increase loyalty among your team and empower them to be part of the solution and take ownership of their actions. Meanwhile, a lack of information only encourages rumors, division, suspicion, and, at worst, can create a mass panic among the team.

SELF-ASSESSMENT

I bet you never thought when starting this journey that you'd be looking at how to improve your sense of negativity, but here we are. But remember—it's all about the balance between positive and negative and how the two can be dance partners.

Think about it like a car battery. Electrons are negatively charged, but a battery needs both positive *and* negative terminals to allow the electric current to flow. The negative electrons are repelled by the negative terminal toward the positive to allow the car to start. In the same way, you must make negativity move in a positive direction to get things moving!

	1. I PAY ATTENTION TO WHEN I HAVE NEGATIVE FEELINGS SO I CAN HAVE THE SOCIAL SUPPORT AROUND ME TO WORK THROUGH THEM.
2	I don't shut down negative emotions or ignore them, but I take a step back to look at the reasons behind them and discuss with trusted members of my relevant Social Support Pods.
1	When negative emotions arise, I usually take the time to think through them, but I don't always discuss them with others.
0	I don't have any consistency with how I handle negative emotions or who I discuss them with.
-1	I only think about or discuss negative emotions when things get so bad I don't know what else to do.
-2	I shut down negative feelings because I see them as a weakness, and I sure as hell am not going to share them with anyone else.

If you're alive at this moment, I can promise negative feelings are going to come up at some point. But the first step in managing a Negative Affect is learning how to process those feelings of stress, anxiety, and so on—and having a Social Support Network who can help you with processing them. Bottling up those emotions or pretending they aren't there is a great way to bring yourself and everyone else down.

	2. I MAKE A HABIT OF BEING "BEST-IMISTIC" TO HELP ME MAKE WISE DECISIONS.
2	I approach both opportunities and problems with a sense of caution, practicing calculated risk.
1	I tend to show more caution in specific areas of my life while being more nonchalant in others.
0	I'm cautious in most areas of my life, but I occasionally get blindsided in moments where I was too trusting.
-1	I'm too busy to take the time to be cautious. I defer as many judgments to others as I possibly can.
-2	All of my decisions are spontaneous rather than taking time to be cautious and lay out the possibilities.

There's nothing wrong with going with your gut on certain things. But part of a healthy pessimism applies to being pessimistic about your decision-making and asking, "Am I reacting out of my own bias or past experience?" All the more reason to take a step back and weigh all the facts so you can do a gut check and feel more confident in your decision.

3. I KNOW HOW TO APPROPRIATELY HARNESS NEGATIVE EXPERIENCES/EMOTIONS TO MOVE FORWARD IN A POSITIVE DIRECTION.

2	When crisis or negativity arises, I am consistently able to convert that into problem-solving fuel, and I encourage others to do the same.
1	I can generally use stress or a negative experience to find the good and feel motivated, but it usually takes me a bit of time and distance from the situation.
0	I'm really only able to harness negative experiences and emotions when there is lots of encouragement from others to do so.
-1	In general, I feel weighed down by negative emotions/ experience; instead of motivating me, they make me feel like I will probably just fail the next time too.
-2	I don't deal with my negative emotions or find the good in past failures. I'd rather pretend they never happened.

Look, we all make mistakes—we all fall short of the mark at some point or have bad things happen to us. But in the wise words of Rafiki from *The Lion King*, "You can either run from it … or *learn* from it." Knowing how to harness those instances, learning from them, and being motivated by them can move you in a positive direction.

	4. EVEN WITH BAD NEWS, I PRACTICE TRANSPARENCY WITH MY TEAM SO THAT WE CAN BE ON THE SAME PAGE, REMAIN CALM AND FOCUSED, AND SOLVE THE PROBLEM.
2	I practice transparency and encourage those around me to do the same with their teams.
1	I'm transparent with those nearest to me and have seen the benefit of how it builds trust and collaboration, but I don't actively encourage it in others.
0	I'm picky about transparency because I struggle with others viewing me as weak or ineffective if they know the whole story.
-1	I'm transparent but only so I can dump my problems on others and get it off my shoulders.
-2	The idea of transparency sounds foolish to me, and I think people would take advantage of me or abandon me if I were to start.

There is a delicate balance with being transparent while also being sensitive to others. You don't want to be like Jim Carrey in *Liar Liar* where a practice of brutal honesty leaves a path of destruction behind you. But you also don't want to be so closefisted about everything that there is no trust between you and your team. You can be open and honest without wearing everything on your sleeve.

5. I'M ABLE TO LOOK AHEAD TO THE FUTURE AND PREPARE FOR PROBLEMS THAT HAVEN'T HAPPENED YET.	
2	When strategy planning, I try to think of worst-case scenarios to help me lay the groundwork to prevent a crisis and protect my team.
1	I'm able to process through old problems to come up with response plans for the future.
0	It's difficult for me to look too far ahead—I'm usually stuck in the week-to-week cycle of problem-solving.
-1	I feel like I'm usually in crisis mode; I can't think about tomorrow because I'm still working on yesterday's problems.
-2	Whatever happens happens. As long as I have a way to get out, everyone else can fend for themselves.

One of the greatest advantages of Negative Affect is the ability to think ahead to worst-case scenarios and strategize to protect others. Whether it's a staffing crisis, financial crisis, or midlife crisis, it's always better to prepare for the worst and be ready. Even if the crisis never comes, at least you've brought some peace of mind to you and your organization to be more effective. Sure, you don't want to operate every moment of the day anticipating the zombie apocalypse or you won't get anything done—but you also don't want to assume that everything will always be sunshine and puppies.

CONCLUSION

I'll be the first to admit you're not going to walk into work every day with a smile. And you're not going to walk out of work every day with a smile either. But you can harness Negative Affect to make you a prepared problem solver … or you can let Negative Affect harness *you* and turn you into either a Debbie Downer or a straight-up jerk.

The relationship between Positive and Negative Affect can be thought of like riding a bicycle. You have to push a negative direction (backward) to move the bike in a positive direction (forward). Ultimately, when you can be honest about your feelings with yourself and others, it can lead you into a place of freedom and opportunity.

CHAPTER 10

FREEDOM

Freedom, in any case, is only possible by constantly struggling for it.
— *ALBERT EINSTEIN*

When I think of freedom, I can't help but think of the Spirit of the Immigrant. I think about my parents and grandparents who immigrated from Italy to Pittsburgh so they could be free and also to provide us—the next generation—with more freedom.

I think of another Italian immigrant who ended up in Pittsburgh, wrestling Hall of Famer Bruno Sammartino, "The Italian Strongman" who held the title of Heavyweight Wrestling Champion twice and would sell out Madison Square Garden a staggering 187 times during his career. But long before his fame, the Sammartino family had to truly fight for their freedom.

Born in the small Italian village of Valla Rocca in 1935 as the youngest of seven, his father immigrated to Pittsburgh in 1939 in the hopes of earning enough money to bring the rest of the family to America. Unfortunately, German soldiers occupied the village and Sammartino's family was forced to flee the town and literally live in a cave.

Sammartino later recalled how his mother would heroically sneak into the village at night and take food out of houses while Nazi soldiers patrolled the streets or lounged in rooms just above the kitchens where she would take whatever she could find.

During this time, several of his siblings tragically died, and then the whole family was discovered by the Nazis. In a scene that feels like it's from a movie, his family was lined up for execution, but mere moments before the trigger was pulled, Allied forces swept in to the rescue.

In 1950, the surviving members of the Sammartino family were finally reunited with his father in Pittsburgh, free from the oppression they had endured.

As if that wasn't enough, his troubles didn't end there. In a way that feels all too familiar from my own story, Bruno was bullied at school. In a true example of taking a negative situation in a positive direction, the bullying inspired him to take up weightlifting so he could gain the confidence to defend himself—and that started him on his incredible journey to become one of the greatest professional wrestlers of all time.

With stories like his, the concept of freedom takes on a new light, doesn't it? Too often we take freedom for granted and see it as an entitlement rather than looking for how we can earn it. Freedom can also be incredibly difficult to measure because unlike generosity, which can be measured in dollars or time donated, freedom is more about one's *experience*.

I find that the experience of freedom is directly related to how confident one feels in the situation they are facing. For example, Bruno

Sammartino had watched his mom stand up to the Nazis—and he knew weightlifting would give him the confidence he needed to face his own bullies. Likewise, your experience of financial freedom will be based on how confident you are that you'll have money in the bank when you pay the bills. As a leader, my experience of freedom at work is dependent on the level of confidence and trust I have in my team.

It's really easy to fall into the trap that freedom is equivalent to control and power, that more freedom means being able to do more of whatever you want. But—spoiler alert—that's a very limited view of what freedom actually is. Having a leadership role may give you more freedom than others, but it also gives you more responsibility and, therefore, the more necessary it is to make calculated risks because the wrong decision could end up costing you—and others—freedom and confidence.

Not to be cliché, but freedom is never free—it comes at a cost. You may feel like you're giving up your freedom if you allow others to have more freedom, but that's also a wrong view. When you focus on helping others build up their confidence and, therefore, how free they feel, it not only makes them happier team members, but gives you more freedom because you're not dictating their every move.

FREEDOM

In the context of the World Happiness Index, freedom can be summarized as how free people feel to make their own life choices. These choices are determined by two aspects: first, that individuals have the *opportunity* to choose, and second, that individuals have the *capacity* to choose. The less opportunity and the less capacity for choices, the less freedom and less happiness.

Diving deeper, Freedom can be broken up into three distinct types: **Social Freedom**, **Psychological Freedom**, and **Potential**

Freedom. With P-HI, well, it's exactly the same. These three types of freedom overlap and intertwine with one another to help determine your overall happiness.

SOCIAL FREEDOM

To go back to Social Support, Social Freedom is all about the opportunity and capacity to build meaningful relationships. The only thing that can make leadership feel less lonely is surrounding yourself with people you trust so that when you're faced with a problem, you have people you can talk to, whether family, coworkers, or mentors.

It also begs the question: Do the people around you feel free to come to you when they are faced with a problem? Do they have the confidence that they can approach you and that you'll listen without judgment? You might have an "open door policy," but if people are afraid to come to you, then it doesn't matter how open that door may be.

PSYCHOLOGICAL FREEDOM

When looking at Psychological Freedom as a leader, the only thing standing in your way is you. As the leader, you've got both the opportunity and capacity to make choices, but maybe you don't feel confident to make those choices. Also, I think it's important for leaders—especially young leaders—to understand that there's a difference between being *confident* and being *condescending*.

True confidence inspires others and helps them build up their own confidence—and they'll want to follow you. False confidence means you might feel pretty good about yourself but only at the expense of others as you talk down to them, demean them, and rob them of any confidence they had. If that's you—congrats! You're a parasite. Eventually, this will turn people away from you as they experience less freedom any time they're around you.

As a leader, you're the only one standing in the way of your own Psychological Freedom, but you need to be aware that you might be standing in the way of someone else's experience of freedom. In other words, are you aware of how psychologically free the people around you are? Or are you so self-focused that you're completely oblivious and assume others have your same level of confidence?

Recently, my friend Kelly went on a hiking trip with seven of her girlfriends, all members of different organizations and different professional levels. The topic of confidence in the workplace came up, and while Kelly's response was, "Heck yeah, I have confidence!" she quickly discovered that was not the experience for the other women in the group. Most said they felt very low confidence, and one of them said she literally feels like collapsing and crying at work because she has *zero* confidence. How sad is that?

One of her friends shared that whenever people heard the sound of their boss's high heels clicking down the hallway, they would turn the other way, close their doors, or even pretend to be on the phone— just so they wouldn't have to deal with her. With every interaction, she was sapping away freedom and confidence from her team to bolster her own ego. That's another kind of Leaderstein—a monster in the workplace no one wants to face.

In basketball, a triple threat stance is a posture where a player can choose to dribble, shoot, or pass. The triple threat stance gives the player a lot of freedom with options. But in the workplace, a triple threat move is when someone calls, emails, then visits your office in person—one, two, three—before you have a chance to respond. Do you know that person? Or are *you* that person? It's great to be a triple threat basketball player, but being a triple threat boss can only result in you robbing your team of psychological freedom and make them want to eat garlic every day in the hope of warding you off.

So as you grow in your Psychological Freedom, it's so important to be attuned to the Psychological Freedom of those around you. How productive is your team going to be if they come in with a mindset of no freedom, no confidence? Where can you mentor others and help them grow in their experience of freedom?

POTENTIAL FREEDOM

This final type of freedom is about how aware you are of the freedoms that you have ahead of you. You don't know what you don't know, after all, and you're ignorant to pretend otherwise. The problem is that a lot of leaders feel like they have to project an omniscient attitude, that they have all the answers. But assuming you know everything doesn't make you more free—it backs you into a corner because it's an unrealistic expectation. In fact, I like to say that, "If you are the smartest person in the room, you're in the wrong room."

Instead, Potential Freedom is more about what you learn over time, the experience and knowledge accumulated over the years. There's a lot of literature out there—whether it's related to leadership, finances, or relationships—that says, "Do this and do that and you'll be successful," which only encourages you to turn your life into a giant checklist. Not to be Captain Obvious again, but Potential Freedom is about *potential*—what is ahead of you, what you can still learn, what you can still experience. Looking ahead and realizing how much more you still have to learn can only serve to motivate you to keep growing.

I'm a big believer that if you hire people smarter than you and just get out of their way, then they're going to end up giving *you* a whole lot more freedom because *they* will experience more freedom.

I once had a hard conversation with one of my staff members that shows all three kinds of freedom colliding together in the best possible way. We had just hired a fantastic, brilliant person to work under this staff member, and one day I asked her, "How are things going so far?"

And she looked at me and said, "Frankly, I feel like an intern."

That's about the worst thing I could hear from an employee—that they don't feel any sense of freedom to do anything except follow the script their boss lays out for them. And she wasn't the first person I'd heard this from, so I knew we had a problem.

So I sat her supervisor down in my office and said, "Listen, I'm getting a lot of feedback about you that in meetings you're not giving people the opportunity to talk. Or, if they do talk, you end up talking over or talking down to them and not taking their suggestions seriously. Look," I explained to him, "if there's any way that you want to lose people, that's it right there."

He was obviously embarrassed to hear this but was completely open and asked, "Well, what do I need to do to fix this?"

I answered, "You need to open up the meeting—and then shut up and let *them* talk."

So then I pulled them into a room together—and I didn't pull any punches—and we discussed how we could fix the situation immediately.

In full transparency, during that meeting with both of them, she said to me, "I've worked for some big CEOs, and you're the first one who's been approachable, showed some common sense, and then acted on it."

Now, I'm not saying all that to pat myself on the back but to make a point:

This woman felt the Social and Psychological Freedom to be confident enough to approach me with the problem. I felt the Social and Psychological Freedom to go to her supervisor and talk to him frankly. He showed the Social and Potential Freedom to receive the feedback and ask how he could fix things.

Now, things could've gone differently. If she hadn't felt confident to approach me with the problem, then I wouldn't have known how bad it really was, and we could've lost some valuable Human Capital if she decided "This isn't worth it—I can work somewhere else." And if he hadn't been receptive and confident that he could change, then I could've also lost him if he decided, "Screw you! How dare you tell me how to lead my team?"

Maybe you're on board with the idea of more freedom for yourself, but you might worry: "What if I give people freedom and they take advantage of it?" My question back would be "What if you *don't* give people freedom? How will that help you as a leader?" And to take it a step further than that, "Why would you *not* want your people to grow in their experience of freedom?"

GROWING INTO FREEDOM

More than ever, I believe that Freedom is essential to growth—for yourself, for your team, and for your organization. This is also where I continue to see the overlap and relationship between freedom and confidence. When you feel freedom in your life, you feel more confident; when you feel more confident, you grow.

There's a scene in the movie *The Gambler* between Mark Wahlberg and John Goodman's characters that sticks with me. Now, I'll edit the quote here to make it a bit more appropriate, but there is a scene where John Goodman's character Frank says, "A wise man's life is based around f*** you."

His point in the scene is stressing that when you are financially secure, you can live your life around the principle of "f*** you," but

I want to modify the quote with a different f-word—that's right—*freedom*. I think that a wise man's life is based around freedom.

What moves are you making to be more financially free? What are you doing to be more professionally free? What are you doing to be more socially free? Mentally free? You get the gist.

When you know where you want to be—free—then you can start taking actions to get there. This is big in "choosing your hard" because it doesn't happen overnight or without a lot of work, but the end game of freedom will make it worth it. There's nothing like making that final credit card payment, or stepping into your dream job, or having the freedom to take your family on the dream vacation.

> **When you feel freedom in your life, you feel more confident; when you feel more confident, you grow.**

Among the younger generation coming into leadership—the millennials and Gen-Zers—I hear a lot about wanting to grow "organically." A lot of times people use this word the wrong way, meaning they want things to happen passively or on their own. Well, guess what? That's not how the world works! Ask any organic farmer out there—you reap what you sow. And it's no different in your professional development, your marriage, or your relationships with others. If you want it to grow, you put in the hard work, and the result is more freedom.

But you don't get Freedom on day one, so you've got to get that idea out of your head. The US founding fathers may have signed the Declaration of Independence on July 4, 1776, but actual freedom from Britain wasn't accomplished until the Treaty of Paris was signed on September 3, 1783—*seven* years later! And there was a lot of *hard* in those seven years.

SELF-ASSESSMENT

Gauging your sense of Freedom can be tricky because maybe you've never thought about it before. Maybe you're the type who really likes things to be black-and-white and have everything spelled out for you. While I'm not that type of person myself, I've known people who feel more free when they are given strict and firm boundaries. Too many blank spaces make them feel out of control. Therefore, it's important to think of this based more on your experience and confidence level, regardless of your preferences.

1. MY ORGANIZATION PROVIDES ME WITH THE OPPORTUNITY TO GROW IN FREEDOM AND CONFIDENCE.	
2	I have plenty of opportunity to grow my Natural Resources and Human Capital so that I can be more confident in my abilities.
1	I have some opportunities to grow my Natural Resources, but I would like to have more.
0	Opportunities for growth are typically thrust upon me. I don't really get much choice in the matter.
-1	There are few opportunities to grow. Any that arise are usually mandatory, regulatory-type trainings rather than focused on growing Human Capital.
-2	There are no opportunities, and I haven't had any kind of training since I started with my organization.

Regardless of whether you ask for opportunities or whether you have a choice in those opportunities, I believe it's important for overall happiness and success that you feel the freedom to pursue them. If you're part of an organization that lands in the -1 or -2 level above, then you have to either create those opportunities for yourself or think really hard about where you really want to be.

	2. I FEEL A STRONG SENSE OF SOCIAL FREEDOM.
2	I can clearly connect my experience of Freedom to my Social Support Network.
1	In general, I have a Social Support Network that helps me experience Freedom, though I know it could go further.
0	I'm aware of how Social Support can help me grow in Freedom, but it's inconsistent in different areas of my life.
-1	My sense of Social Freedom is mostly absent.
-2	Not only is Social Freedom absent, but I feel that those around me take freedom from me.

If this feels a lot like what you scored back in Social Support, you're not wrong! There should be a huge overlap between your sense of Social Freedom and the strength of your support pods around you. Hopefully, you've identified how you can strengthen those relationships, which will automatically lead to a higher score here too.

	3. I FEEL A STRONG SENSE OF PSYCHOLOGICAL FREEDOM.
2	I feel confident in my ability to take calculated risks, voice my opinions, and act freely in a way that also encourages others to be more free.
1	I typically feel confident in the workplace and my ability to act independently, but I don't always think about how to encourage this in others.
0	My sense of Psychological Freedom varies day to day and depends largely on the moods and actions of others.
-1	I don't feel confident most days in the workplace or my working relationships and feel like I am walking a tightrope to keep myself safe.
-2	Not only do I not feel confident, but Psychological Freedom is discouraged and prohibited. Everything has to be "by the book" and creativity is discouraged.

Again, some people feel more free when given a lot of structure, and that's okay if that's you. But if so, you have to remember that may not be the case with everyone around you, and as a leader, it's your job to be aware of not just your Psychological Freedom but those around you. Assuming that everyone needs the same level of structure can hurt the trust you are trying to build and rob confidence from others.

4. I FEEL A STRONG SENSE OF POTENTIAL FREEDOM.	
2	I have a clear and strategic idea of where I still need to grow and how I can get there.
1	I'm aware that I "don't know what I don't know," but I need to become more strategic in how to fill in those gaps.
0	I generally don't think about my potential until it's brought up by others.
-1	Most days, I don't feel like I have the capacity to think of my potential.
-2	At the moment, I don't have any sense for what my potential is or how to get there.

One really cool thing about this question is that it's more about your awareness. So perhaps you scored low on Question 1 because your organization gives you limited opportunity to grow, but maybe your personal sense of Potential Freedom is high, which allows you to score well here. If that's you, then you can start to think of how you can bridge the gap between the two by either creating those opportunities for yourself or moving to a new organization that will be aligned with your sense of Potential Freedom.

5. I'M ACTIVELY LOOKING FOR HOW I CAN ENCOURAGE FREEDOM IN OTHERS.

2	I use my Freedom as a leader to provide others with the opportunity to grow in their confidence.
1	I use my influence to grow those immediately around me in their potential and perceived freedom but not on an organizational level.
0	My efforts in growing others' Freedom is inconsistent and usually based on problem areas that have been identified.
-1	In general, I don't make the Freedom of others a focus because I'm concerned about how others will take advantage of it.
-2	Why would I want others to feel more free? They just need to do things the way I say and leave it at that. If they want to feel free, they can leave.

This question is a lot like Question 1, but instead of looking at how your organization impacts your Freedom, look at how your Freedom impacts your organization. Not to beat a dead horse, but it's a limited view to only think about *your* sense of Freedom. A true leader knows how to wield their sense of freedom to grow it in others.

CONCLUSION

One thing I love about the story of the late Bruno Sammartino is that he didn't allow his struggles for freedom to end with himself or his family. He used his influence in wrestling to look at how he could give back to the sport, to younger wrestlers, and increase their opportunities. He and his wife also started the Bruno and Carol Sammartino Foundation working to "eradicate hunger and homelessness"[16] in Western Pennsylvania.

---

16 Bruno and Carol Sammartino Foundation Mission Statement, accessed March 20, 2021, brunosammartinofoundation.com.

One can see how his early life—the lack of literal freedom by living in a cave and surviving off of what his mother could scavenge—was clearly connected to his desire to give back and create more freedom, confidence, and opportunity for others. As your experience of freedom increases, it should also increase the desire to give back and be more generous to others.

CHAPTER 11

GENEROSITY

*My father always taught me to appreciate what you're
fortunate to have and give back to those who need it.*
— *DAN MARINO*

Starting kindergarten is an exciting event for parents, children, and
teachers alike because it can set the course for a life filled with curiosity,
learning, and—hopefully—making a lasting difference on this earth.
For me, I remember being excited but also very anxious—centered
around meeting new friends, riding the bus, and being away from my
parents *plus* the anxiety of having to communicate in English.

Even though this happened forty years ago, I can still
remember there was an initial assessment on how well you knew
your letters and their association with various pictures. The test
was very straightforward: there were twenty-six pictures with a
small line under each one, and we were supposed to write the first
letter for the object of the picture. For example, if the picture was

that of a dog, you would write the letter *D*. Pretty easy, right? I mean, this wasn't the MCAT.

Reflecting on this, I realized this was the first written examination I had ever taken in my life. My teacher, Mrs. Wolfe, handed the tests out and as I looked at all the pictures I thought, "I got this." I had no problem with following the directions—the real challenge for me was interpretation. Still, I quickly completed the test and turned it in. In fact, I think I was one of the first to complete it—surely, there would be bonus points for speed. Mrs. Wolfe smiled as she took the paper from me and, at that moment, I was convinced I was going to fit in and be just fine.

Later that week, my parents received a call from Mrs. Wolfe, requesting a parent-teacher meeting. I was sure she was going to tell my parents I was a genius and should go straight to first grade. As we arrived for our meeting, my optimism quickly disappeared when Mrs. Wolfe held out my test and proceeded to tell my parents that I didn't get a single answer correct.

Wait … what?

She told my parents that she did not have an explanation for the results and suggested I be tested for a learning disability.

Then my father asked to see the test. My parents knew little English, but my father was a little better since he was a bus driver and had to use English more. After a moment's examination, he smiled, looked at Mrs. Wolfe, and said, "These answers are all right."

At that moment, I am certain she thought the entire family must have a learning deficiency. But he proceeded to show her that all the pictures were answered with the correct letter, except they were answered in Italian. I wish I could have taken a picture of her face at that moment.

As the realization dawned on her, Mrs. Wolfe replied, "I will never grade a test the same way again." From that moment on, she knew that not only did I have the capability to learn but that I was able to do so in two languages.

Frankly, I think it would've been easy for most teachers to just write me off based on the test results, saying, "This one's just dumb—he can't learn." Instead, she invested extra time with me to help me improve my English. Even when I moved on to first grade, she was there to help me. And then when I moved on to second grade, she was still there. She showed a level of unparalleled generosity with her time to make sure that I could succeed in life.

Throughout my life, whether in business or personal settings, that one moment with my parents and Mrs. Wolfe continues to resonate with me. In addition to donating her time to teach me English, she also taught me to never judge anyone by a resume or by their quiet nature but to talk to people, get to know them and their story—and you might find that they are capable of much more than what you can see on the outside.

She passed away in 2003, but I'll never forget the impact she's made on my life. We often think of being generous in terms of monetary donations but, in my case, the generosity of Mrs. Wolfe's time was priceless and helped guide me to who I am today.

The way I see it, Generosity is the peak, the pinnacle, of happiness. Mrs. Wolfe became a part of my Social Support when she decided to talk to my parents and invest in my well-being. Instead of seeing my situation as an obstacle, she brought a Positive Affect to teaching me, guiding me through a negative situation that helped me learn how to persevere and prepare so that I could have

Generosity is the peak, the pinnacle, of happiness.

the freedom to pursue whatever path I would choose. I can say with confidence that's not only what made her a successful teacher, but that's also what brought her happiness.

And this isn't just an isolated incident. Research conducted by the Greater Good Science Center at UC Berkeley showed a strong link between generosity and happiness. They found that "while popular culture may imply that happiness comes from focusing on yourself, research suggests the opposite: Being generous can make you happier."[17]

My life is filled with similar examples of people who have been generous to me in many different ways, all of which have contributed to the person I am today. Happiness and success should never terminate with yourself—but instead should overflow into those around you. In sports terms, it's not just about winning the game but becoming the coach or team sponsor to help others win their games too.

GENEROSITY

In the World Happiness Index, Generosity is gauged by how much a nation is able to lend support to others. This can typically be quantified as foreign aid for specific services or programs that need to be developed, or sending manpower and talent like troops or medical professionals to assist in a crisis response.

With P-HI, it's very much the same, though the true value is not measured in the *amount* of what is given but rather in the *intention* behind the Generosity. Back when I first became CEO, we were going through some major changes to improve things and had a big fundraiser. I'll never forget when I had one of our employees come up to me and hand me an envelope with seventy-five cents in it and say, "Here's my donation—I'm sorry that's all I can give."

I stood there and thought, "Holy crap … here's a person making twelve, maybe thirteen dollars an hour while I know people making

---

17   Summer Allen, "The Science of Generosity," John Templeton Foundation, May 2018, 23, https://ggsc.berkeley.edu/images/uploads/GGSC-JTF_White_Paper-Generosity-FINAL.pdf.

seven figures who have never donated a penny to us." I know she was probably embarrassed by the small amount she was giving, but it felt like a million bucks to me because I knew she was giving it out of the kindness of her heart and her passion for our mission.

I've seen people donate $10,000 just to get other people off their backs. I know it; they know it. But giving out of wealth isn't the same as giving from the heart. If you make a huge donation but then turn around and ask, "Now what building are you going to name after me?" that's not Generosity—that's just ego.

The kind of generosity that brings happiness should never be a transaction. Instead, the way I see it, there are three types of Generosity: **Time**, **Talent**, and **Treasure**. Leaders should be the first to recognize that you haven't found any success on your own, so you should look really hard at how you can be generous in all three.

TIME

For starters, everybody has the ability to be generous with their time. Maybe it's by lending a hand to a work project. Maybe it's by listening to someone unpack the difficult day they just had. Maybe it's turning the phone off and spending uninterrupted time with your family. Maybe it's mentoring or teaching. But it doesn't take any special talent to give your time.

Does that mean it's always easy to do? No, but that's part of what makes giving your time so generous. After all, no matter how much money you have, you can't buy time. It's an incredibly valuable asset, so I'd *absolutely* agree it's a sacrifice to give it up. In that sense, time might just be the most valuable thing you can ever give to someone.

To this day, Mrs. Wolfe's generosity has inspired me to be more generous with my time and to look for how I can be a teacher to others. In fact, I recently got two separate emails in the same week from individuals looking for mentors for students and I said, "Yes, I'm happy to talk to them." I don't say this to pat myself on the back—rather, I see this as a small way that I can pay forward the generosity that Mrs. Wolfe showed me all those years ago.

TALENT

Now, when you think about Talent, you have to think back to those Natural Resources you've already identified. How can you use those to not just benefit yourself but add value for others? Talents aren't meant to be kept to yourself but shared for everyone's benefit. Think about it—what if Andrea Bocelli only sang in the shower? What if Steven Spielberg only made home movies? What if Garth Brooks only played guitar in his garage alone? What a shame that would be!

Everyone has a God-given talent, and I believe everyone's given an opportunity to share it with others. But here's the thing about opportunity—you have to be actively looking for it. And that's key with being generous with your talent in particular—you should be looking for the opportunity to share it. Maybe you've let fear keep you from doing so, but remember—no one ever accomplished anything great by backing down from fear but by facing it.

Maybe it's not fear stopping you, though. Maybe it's selfishness which leads you to hoard your talent for yourself. But your talent could make the difference in someone else's life. When Dr. Thomas Starzl started the transplant program at UPMC, it wasn't so that the hospital could have a monopoly on transplant surgeons. Instead, he shared his talent and his time so that aspiring transplant doctors could go out and save lives all over the country and the world.

TREASURE

Ultimately, being generous with your Time and Talent should naturally culminate in being generous with your Treasure … that is, your bank account. This doesn't mean you throw around cash willy-nilly but that you give to a cause that you're passionate about, something that will bring you ongoing happiness and even purpose.

By the way, your passion may or may not align with your talents. Back to Garth Brooks, you might think that, given his particular talent, he would donate his treasure to something music-related. Instead, his foundation Teammates for Kids supports pediatric hospitals, provides sports and recreation programs for inner city children, and opens up educational opportunities for the underprivileged. Because he's passionate about those things, he uses the opportunities opened by his talent to not only be generous with *his* treasure but also inspire others to be generous with their treasure too.

So maybe you don't have the means to create an entire foundation, but you *can* identify what causes you care for the most and give something back to the world. Whatever you do, it should come from the heart and should help others on the stairway to success.

Out of respect for them, I won't mention their names, but there is one family in particular who gives our organization some incredible gifts every year that combine their Time, Talent, and Treasure. I've reached out to them and asked them, "Hey, how can I honor you? Can we recognize you in some way?" And their response is always the same: "Don't you dare let anyone know about this." They get more satisfaction and happiness out of the act of giving itself and knowing that it will improve the lives of others. For them, any personal recognition would taint the experience, and that alone is a humbling thought that challenges me in my own efforts to be generous.

HAND IN HAND

I think there should be both overlap and a tag-team approach to Time, Talent, and Treasure. You don't graduate from one to another, but you continually look for ways to be generous in all three. For example, you can combine Time and Treasure by volunteering to help out with a fundraiser. Or you could combine Time and Talent by passing on your knowledge to the next generation.

In fact, that's why our employee recognition program I've mentioned before incorporates each participant getting to shadow and be mentored by members of our C-Suite team. I want my leadership team to be generous in giving their time and talent because the participants will be our next generation of leaders. Ultimately, this results in us being more generous with our Treasure too, either by promoting them to higher-paid jobs—or setting them up to be prepared for higher-paid jobs elsewhere if that's what they decide to do.

Some may see that as foolish and say, "But why invest so much into people who might end up leaving you?" And my response is, "Well, what if they don't leave me? Do you think I really want a mediocre staff that will stick around for a long time but achieve little, or do you think I want an exceptional staff who adds value to the organization for however long they stay?" I think it's pretty obvious. Give me a small team of exceptional individuals over a huge staff filled with mediocrity any day of the week.

Above all, I can't stress enough that Generosity must be others-centered. That's why Generosity—the pinnacle of P-HI—and Productivity—the peak of P-GDP—go hand in hand. Where the heart of Productivity is about *doing* your best and inspiring others to do their best, the heart of Generosity is about *giving* the best of yourself to help others be their best.

As Brett Steenbarger observes, "Teams with high generosity/gratitude are simply more productive than other teams ... Successful teams go out of their way to appreciate the contributions of members. This creates a culture of kindness and giving, but also a culture of enhanced productivity."[18] In other words, there is a clear link between Generosity and Productivity. As you measure one, you measure the other. As you grow one, you grow the other.

SELF-ASSESSMENT

So here we are … our final set of questions that will help you complete the picture of your Personal Happiness Index. As I've mentioned before, keep in mind that true Generosity has to be linked to generous motivation—giving that occurs not out of obligation or guilt but out of an overflow of personal happiness to see others be happy and successful.

1. I AM ABLE TO RECOGNIZE AND APPRECIATE THE WAYS OTHERS HAVE BEEN GENEROUS TO ME, WHICH INSPIRES ME TO BE GENEROUS WITH OTHERS.	
2	I can clearly identify situations in my life in which people have shown generosity to me, and I actively look for opportunities to pay it forward.
1	I am able to identify moments when others have been generous to me, and I feel inspired to do the same, but I am not always consistent in looking for opportunities.
0	I know others have been generous to me, but I haven't given active thought to how this has impacted me.
-1	I haven't thought much about how I've been the recipient to the generosity of others, but maybe I should start.
-2	I don't commit any thought to acts of generosity toward me. If I have something, it's because I've earned it.

---

18   Brett Steenbarger, "Generosity and Peak Performance," Forbes.com, April 16, 2018, https://www.forbes.com/sites/brettsteenbarger/2018/04/16/generosity-and-peak-performance/?sh=74429e7b144a.

I believe we live in a world today where many feel entitled to receiving generosity and where generosity is often taken for granted. But first, I think it's important to personalize how the generosity of others has impacted you. If you rank on the lower end of this question, then my two cents is that you take some time to do an Appreciation Exercise by listing out times that others have been generous to you, whether it was something life-altering or just the small act of kindness from yesterday.

2. I AM GENEROUS WITH MY TIME.	
2	I actively look for ways that I can be generous with my Time, both in my professional and personal life.
1	Generally speaking, I try to be generous with my Time, but I tend to do so more in one area of my life than another.
0	I'm not sure whether I'm generous with my Time or not. I guess it depends on my mood that day.
-1	If I give up my Time to someone, it's usually out of a sense of guilt or obligation, and I commit minimally.
-2	I'm not going to give my Time to anyone unless it's clear to me that I get something out of it.

If you're a leader, I believe it's important to be open-handed with your time because that's *why* you're in leadership—to be there for others. In fact, the late Jack Welch once said, "The single most important attribute of leadership is generosity." Despite that, I've had multiple staff who have told me that I'm the first CEO they have met who has invited them into my office and spent time asking them about their day. That doesn't make me feel good—it makes me feel sad. While yes, I know you've got commitments and appointments to keep, your greatest commitment in the workplace should be to your staff. Time spent investing in them is never time wasted.

3. I AM GENEROUS WITH MY TALENT.	
2	I get great happiness out of sharing my Talent with others and look for opportunities where my talents can improve someone else's life.
1	I definitely enjoy sharing my Talent with others, though I need to be more active in looking for opportunities to do so.
0	I like sharing my Talent sometimes, especially when it gets me some attention.
-1	I don't really look for opportunities to share my Talent and get kind of embarrassed when people notice.
-2	My Talent is mine. I don't really see how sharing it will make me or anyone else happier.

Going back to P-GDP, your Natural Resources gain more value when they are shared with others. While it's easy for people to put emphasis on artistic talents, those are not the only ones out there. You may have a talent for connecting with others, for giving advice, for accounting, and so on. If you're feeling untalented, go back to the list you made way back in chapter 2 and start looking for opportunities to exercise those talents more for the good of others.

4. I AM GENEROUS WITH MY TREASURE.	
2	I regularly donate money to causes that I'm passionate about and look for other opportunities to give back to others.
1	I am at least semi-regular in donating to causes I care about, though I know I could probably do more.
0	I donate money to different causes on occasion but with little consistency or intentional thought into the specific causes.
-1	If I do give money to a cause, it's typically out of a sense of guilt or obligation.
-2	I'll donate if I can justify it as a tax write-off. Otherwise, it's my money until I die.

Remember a long time ago when we revisited the cliché but true expression that "money can't buy happiness"? Well, it's time to revisit that again. What do your finances say about your Generosity in regards to Treasure? If someone were to deep dive into your bank statement, would they be able to pinpoint the causes you're passionate about? Do you give for attention or out of guilt—or because it brings you joy to help others?

5. I'M ACTIVELY LOOKING FOR AND CREATING OPPORTUNITIES TO ENCOURAGE GENEROSITY IN OTHERS.	
2	I use my role as a leader to create opportunities for Generosity among our team.
1	I occasionally encourage Generosity in others, though I could be more intentional in creating opportunities.
0	I may encourage Generosity every now and then but not with much rhyme or reason.
-1	I can see why it's important to be generous, but I've given little thought to how to encourage others to be generous.
-2	If people want to be generous, good for them. I don't see why they need my help with that.

Now, a caveat: don't be a hypocrite. Only preach it if you practice it. So if you're not scoring well in Generosity yourself, I think it's going to be hard for you to encourage it in others. But that's the ultimate goal with Generosity: if you can see the link between how the generosity of others has impacted you, then it's part of your role to now inspire it in others. There are lots of ways to encourage this on your team. Maybe it's by planning special birthday surprises for team members and including everyone in the process. Maybe you can find a fundraiser for your team to participate in, like a 5K walk for a charitable cause. It's these simple steps that can help you practice a life of generosity and encourage it in others.

In fact, I'd encourage you to not just take this piece of the assessment for yourself but to give the assessment to your team and ask them to assess you (anonymously, of course) so that you can get a better picture of how generous you truly are. This may reveal blind spots where you can be more giving, especially in terms of your Time and Talent. While they may not know the full extent of your financial giving, of course, they may judge your Treasure score based on how many times you do things like bring breakfast for the team or give small bonuses like gift cards. Compare the scores they give you to how you score yourself and it may reveal something you never noticed about yourself.

CONCLUSION

We live in a culture that's constantly asking, "What's in it for me?" In that extreme, you never give unless it's a transaction, and you know what you're going to get out of it—and I just don't count that as true giving. But you also don't have to go to the other extreme where you sell everything you own and become a monk. Unless, of course, that's what makes you happy. In that case, monk away. As Dr. Robert Puff, host of the Happiness Podcast writes, "Generosity doesn't need to border on martyrdom to be effective. Helping others, in any way that we can, is enough to lead us toward a brighter tomorrow."[19]

And now it's time to figure out what that brighter tomorrow looks like for you. Where in your life and as a leader can you be more generous? Because even if you scored high here and already know the benefits of how Generosity has brought you happiness, you now get

---

19   Robert Puff, "Study Shows Generous Behavior Leads to Increased Happiness," *Psychology Today*, December 5, 2017, https://www.psychologytoday.com/us/blog/meditation-modern-life/201712/study-shows-generous-behavior-leads-increased-happiness.

the challenge of maintaining it and taking it to the next level. The truly great are not measured by what they gain but what they give.

None of this is easy. I told you from the beginning it wouldn't be. But it's worth it because this is about way more than just having a great ROI and keeping shareholders happy. Life is bigger than work, bigger than your job title, bigger than your bank account. Life is what happens between the laughter, tears, and thoughts.

PERSONAL HAPPINESS INDEX SCORE

Just as we did with P-GDP, take a moment to add up all of your scores from chapters 7 through 11, and you'll have your complete Personal Happiness Index. Depending on the total, you'll know which "bucket" of development you're in for P-HI:

INSTRUCTIONAL LEAGUE: -50 TO 0

Yes, you have work to do, but don't give up. You have identified some areas of unhappiness so that you can better define and grow into happiness.

MINOR LEAGUE: 0 TO +34

Like with P-GDP, this is not a bad place to be. The key here, though, is to maintain where you are strong while you improve the areas where you're still lacking.

MAJOR LEAGUE: +35 TO +50

Congrats! You're on your way to truly understanding what brings you Happiness. From here, your goal is to sustain that level and look for ways to be generous and help others pursue happiness.

THE END IS JUST THE BEGINNING

Here's the deal: I've learned a lot of these things the hard way. I don't see myself as an expert—I see myself as someone who's been open to learning, especially from my mistakes. I chose my hard, and that has shaped my own journey as a leader.

I won't go through all the sordid details, but my first experience in management wasn't great to say the least. For one, I smooth-talked my way into the position over people with more experience than myself by manufacturing skills and experience that I hadn't really developed yet and making myself out to be something that I wasn't. As you can imagine, that came back to bite me. Hard.

I was trying to take an elevator to success and basing that success on a job title and higher pay. So while I thought I was a bad a$$ because I was making a whopping 10 percent more than my staff, they weren't exactly fans of the strategy I had used to get the job. They turned resentful—and then rebellious. Looking back, I can't blame them. Turns out, without their support, there was no way I was going to be successful since a manager's success is completely dependent on the success of the team.

Long story short, it was my own fault that the leadershi* hit the fan: my promotion didn't last long, and I had to swallow the bitter pill of humility. My lesson learned, I chose to look on the bright side: I was able to keep working for a great organization in the field of healthcare, and I had discovered where my gaps were so I knew where I needed to grow.

I needed to refocus on my Natural Resources and grow my Human Capital. I needed to establish a Personal Infrastructure that would give me more Freedom to exercise my gifts and pursue my passion. I needed to improve my Low-Tech human touch and build my Social Support. I needed to be more positive, more cautious, and definitely more generous.

And that's been the whole point of figuring out your Personal GDP and your Personal Happiness Index. As leaders, we're more likely to manage and address the things we can measure, so having a gauge of your P-GDP and P-HI helps you pinpoint where you need to focus your attention or sustain any success you are experiencing.

My hope is that these measurements will be something you return to year after year as a state of the *you*-nion and help you determine if you are headed the right direction. The process of writing this book has made me reevaluate myself and reminded me that being a leader is a continuous journey, and I have to constantly keep working at it.

Because the end of this book is just the beginning. Every day is a new chance to lead. There is a difference between reading and learning and learning and applying. I hope that in reading this book you've learned what you need to apply to become a happy and successful leader, but if nothing else, I want to dedicate the next few thoughts to some key takeaways:

DOES SUCCESS BRING HAPPINESS, OR DOES HAPPINESS BRING SUCCESS?

Great and effective leaders are very similar to artists in that money and success are best viewed not as the end goals in themselves but as natural results of loving what you do and pursuing your passion. Figuring out what makes you happy is not the destination but the fuel for success.

DISCOVER WHO YOU ARE

In an identity-driven culture, it's easy to put your identity into a specific box:

"I'm a boss."

"I'm an athlete."

"I'm a parent."

"I'm a spouse."

But those are layers of who you are, not your entire identity. I think your identity has to go deeper to the values that shape how you see yourself and how you see the world. It's those deep-seated values that can bring clarity and definition to your life, no matter what your passion is. While aspects of your identity may shift over time, it's important to be able to look back, remember your roots, and see how your past has impacted your present.

For me, it's those values of the Spirit of the Immigrant, the Heart of the Warrior, and the Soul of the Servant. Those values were instilled in me by my parents and grandparents and continue to shape the core of who I am, especially in the kind of leader I want to be in both my personal *and* professional life. The starting point for happiness and success has to be an honest understanding of who you are. Not to get too philosophical or psychological, but identifying and understanding who you are will guide you better along your path than any simple checklist could ever do.

It also means not just becoming a clone of another leader or taking bits and pieces of other leaders to become a Leaderstein, but really embracing your uniqueness to become the best version of yourself.

DON'T BE A TRIPLE THREAT

Using a triple threat move on the basketball court is a very positive thing for the player, but being a triple threat boss is a negative because it means you rob others of freedom by hounding them and micromanaging them. Fans flock to the triple threat player for an autograph … people avoid the triple threat boss. Developing a team that trusts you begins with entrusting them with the freedom to harness their Natural Resources and Human Capital. That will never happen if all they want to do is hide from you.

PRODUCTIVE AND GENEROUS

Remember that the culmination of P-GDP is Productivity and the pinnacle of P-HI is Generosity. Both are achieved through creating, measuring, and understanding each of the factors in your personal economic framework and your personal happiness attributes. It's not a buffet where you get to pick and choose which ones to partake in but a sum of all of them working together in harmony.

NATURAL RESOURCES

We're all different and possess varying sets of skills and tools that we either inherit or acquire over time. Often, these are rooted in what we are passionate about, but only you can determine what those resources are and then build upon them. You can be mediocre at a lot of things, so shift your focus to where you can be truly excellent.

If you're not sure where to start, go back to the exercise from Natural Resources where we discussed researching, understanding, and embracing your Work Lineage. Don't just find out who your "work ancestors" were, but find out what they did to make a lasting impact. Not only will you glean direction from this work ancestry, but it should create a vision for the impact you want to make and the legacy you want to leave behind.

ANYONE CAN LEAD!

Remember the Pixar movie *Ratatouille*? If you've never seen it, you're missing out. It's about a rat with a love for gourmet cooking following in the footsteps of a famous chef who lives by the mantra, "Anyone can cook!" I believe the same to be true with leadership: anyone can lead!

I've seen firsthand that no two leaders are the same and that successful leaders can come from anywhere. After all, a cookbook doesn't have just one recipe; there are lots of recipes to choose from. So it's not about following someone else's recipe so you can be force-fitted into a persona of leadership traits but understanding yourself well enough to know how to grow organically—that is, by investing in your Natural Resources and building a Social Support Network.

SETTLING THE SCORE

If you took the SAT, then you know that your final score was made up from two scores: your Evidence-Based Reading and Writing score

211

and your Math score. We're going to do the same thing here now with your results, so take a moment to look back at each factor and look at your measurements for each:

PERSONAL GDP
Natural Resources
Health and Infrastructure
Human Capital
Technology
Productivity
PERSONAL HAPPINESS INDEX
Social Support
Positive Affect
Negative Affect
Freedom
Generosity

So add up all these scores the way we did in both P-GDP and P-HI to get your final tally on where you land with the combination of the two. From there, you can determine your final "bucket" in your leadership journey through the adjusted scale that combines both sets of values:

Instructional League: -100 to -1
Minor League: 0 to +79
Major League: +80 to +100

Now, a big thing I want to impress on you is that numbers will never tell the whole story, and you are not your score. You need to be able to separate who you are as an individual from your score and look at it for what it is: a gauge that helps you determine the actions and steps you need to take. You could score a +100, but if you either weren't honest with yourself or don't put in the work to maintain that score, then it doesn't help you or anyone around you.

If you scored low overall, I don't want you to be discouraged but rather to turn that negative number into a positive. They say it took Edison ten thousand tries to get the design of the lightbulb right, after all, and even though Ty Cobb holds the record for the highest batting average at 0.366, that still means that he missed more than he hit.

Just as you have to explain the *why* behind the numbers in any report you present to a supervisor or a board, you need to do the same thing here. What is the *why* behind the number? Why did you score low? Why did you score in the middle? Why did you score high? The answers are more important than the number.

The story behind your score presents you with two choices: to improve or settle. Settling for your score means that you will let that score define who you are which could lead you down a path of lukewarm mediocrity. Or you can let it point you in the right direction to what makes you happy, what gets you out of bed in the morning, what inspires and influences you.

MAKE THE CHOICE

It all comes back to this: you have to choose your hard. You can choose the hard of unhappiness and mediocrity or make the hard decisions and put in the hard work that will lead you to happiness and success. The worst thing you can do is nothing and to just look at this as another checklist that you've finished and move on with no impact and no plan.

The best thing you can do? Pretty much anything! To quote the legendary baseball catcher and coach Yogi Berra, "When you come to a fork in the road, take it." In other words, standing still isn't an option. It gets you nowhere. Even if you take the wrong fork, at least you made a choice to move forward, and you can always learn from the experience to get back on the right track. I love this perspective shift because it means that in life, there are no regrets or mistakes, only adventures and lessons.

Grover Cleveland was voted out of the job of president of the US in 1884 and was reelected in 1888. Walt Disney's first animation company went bankrupt in 1921. J. K. Rowling's first *Harry Potter* book was rejected twelve times before it was published. Michael Jordan was cut from his high school basketball team. These ends were not really the end. They were beginnings, forks in the road on the way to happiness and success. When adversity came along, each of them found a way to break the cycle and turn it into part of their success story.

If you haven't already done it, identify specific actions you can start today to grow. Maybe it's finding a mentor to expand upon your Social Support Network. Maybe it's signing up for that branding class you've been putting off and making excuses for. Maybe it's leaving a miserable job that pays the bills to pursue a career that you're truly passionate about. Whatever it is, the choice is before you, and no one is going to make it for you.

I don't think it's a stretch to say that everyone wants to be happy. Most people just don't know how to get there. Today, you have a better picture of how to get there and the choices that can take you there. The end is just the beginning, and it's entirely possible that your best days are still ahead.

ACKNOWLEDGMENTS

I would like to acknowledge all those individuals who inspired and influenced me personally in the journey to writing this book:

Kelly Hanna, for her support and honest input throughout the process.

Jonathan, for his patience and ability to work through my words and concepts.

Joe, for capturing the essence of my family roots and heritage and memorializing them in such profound and expressive words.

Throughout my career, I have been fortunate to have many mentors who have given many words of wisdom from which I learned so much. I cannot begin to mention all of them, but you know who you are, and I'm forever grateful for you.

Last but not least, the folks at Advantage Media for believing in my concept and bringing it to life—thank you.

ABOUT THE AUTHOR

Nick Vizzoca is a Pittsburgh native, first-generation son of Italian immigrants, and survivor of childhood cancer. A twenty-plus year veteran in healthcare in C-level positions, Nick is a sought-after speaker, serves on boards, and is a philanthropist for multiple causes. Never one to sugarcoat things, he is often consulted by other leaders on everything from employee engagement to crisis management in his never-ending personal mission to better the lives of others. In his free time, you will find him with his wife and three kids, who all enjoy cheering on the Steelers, Penguins, and Pirates. To learn more, please visit www.nickvizzoca.com.